Love eternal Love

Cover design by Michael Avellino
Cover photograph: Couple on Beach at Sunset by IOFOTO / Canva.com

ISBN: 9798358773752 (Trade paperback)

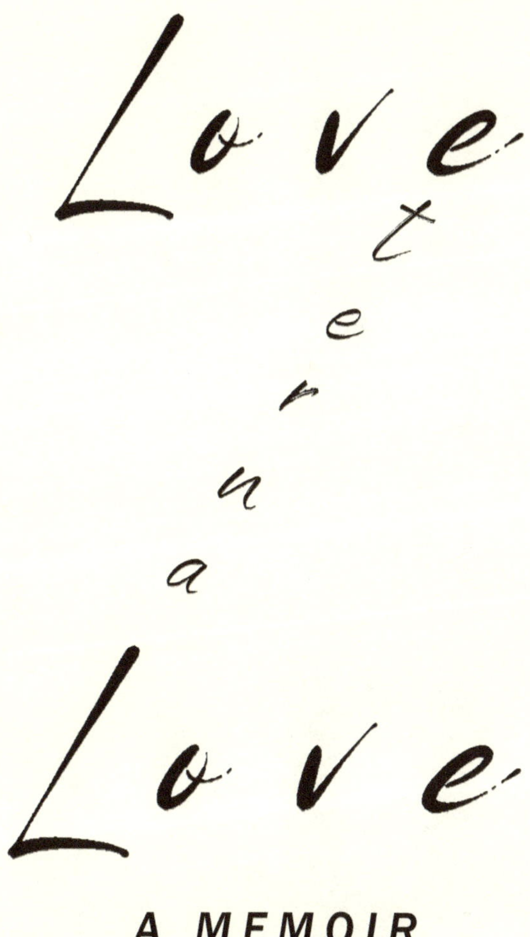

A MEMOIR

MICHAEL AVELLINO

Preface

It's October 25th, 2020, and I just started writing this memoir. I don't have a diary, per say, but I do have cards, letters, poetry, photos, emails, LP/45rpm records, an audio cassette tape I made years ago, and mementos. They've provided a timeline for me, covering the last 40+ years. I kept them because I understood, even then, how special this relationship was. Besides, I'm a hopeless romantic and a sentimental fool… always have been and always will be.

I have a story to tell you about a young boy's dreams, his coming of age, falling in love, and the eventual hard realities he faced. It covers nearly forty-five years up to this point. It's heartwarming. It's heartbreaking. It might make you laugh here and there, and it might bring some tears to your eyes.

It's about two people whose love for each other never left their hearts. It's also about a bond between them that transcends both time and distance. They both made choices and decisions at certain points in their lives that would affect their relationship. As of right now, I can't say with any certainty that the story I'm about to tell you is over. It all depends on your personal beliefs.

Introduction

In the fall of 1967, I was a twelve-year old kid who loved playing baseball and hanging out with his friends. I just started junior high school. Life was good. Life was simple.

A new TV show debuted that fall. It was a western genre show which was very popular in those days. "The High Chaparral" had a diverse and talented cast of actors, including many who were Hispanic, since the show was set in Arizona after the Civil War. There was one actress in particular that I really came to admire. Her name was Linda Cristal who played Victoria Cannon. Although she had a real Spanish accent, Ms. Cristal's heritage was actually French and Italian, and she was born and raised in South America.

Her portrayal of a strong, confident, loving, and loyal woman made quite an impression on me…not to mention, she was really good-looking with long dark hair, and I loved that Spanish accent! In the show, her father's character's name was "Don Sebastian Montoya". There are some odd coincidences in my story, one which relates to what I just mentioned. It can make one wonder sometimes where the coincidences end, and unexplainable statistical improbabilities begin.

That show was on for four seasons. By the time it finished its run, I was not quite yet sixteen years old. Ms. Cristal, *Victoria*, had cemented in me the idea of what the perfect woman, for me anyway, should be. I had no idea how her character had really influenced me until 1976.

I was a good kid. I was the oldest grandchild on both sides of the family, so I was expected to set an example for my younger brother and my cousins. I got to sit around the table with the grown-ups and be seen and not heard. I listened to my parents. I was clean-cut. I didn't get into trouble. I got good grades in school. I worked hard, and I played hard.

I loved baseball and wanted to maybe be a pro someday, but I wasn't nearly good enough. I could run, and as it turned out, that was my ticket to college. In high school I was 6'2", 145lbs, and very competitive in track and cross country at both my county and state levels. My freshman year in college our Cross Country team won the National Championship. So, there were some successes in my personal life by the time I was eighteen years old.

Success with girls? Not so much.

I was a very big fan of actor Errol Flynn—that swashbuckling, womanizing, handsome epitome of male virility. I suppose I liked his movies because he was everything that I wasn't when it came to women. I was very shy and introverted and couldn't hold a five-minute conversation with a girl. I had one date; yes, one date in high school, and it was a total flop.

I'd had two one-night stands along the way, and I dated three or four more girls my first two years in college through 1975. I dated one of those girls about a dozen times and never got past first-base with her, but I liked her a lot.

Connie and I stayed in touch as pen pals through 1977. In January of 1976, we agreed that I would visit her on Memorial Day weekend, where she was living in another state. I still had feelings for her and was looking forward to it, since we hadn't seen each other since May of '75 when classes ended.

Then there are those pesky coincidences. There have been quite a few that occurred especially in these last few years, and I've come to believe that maybe they were more than just coincidences. Both the Bible and a quote from Shakespeare's play Hamlet have always made me wonder if this world we're born into and we die in is just the beginning of our existence in this universe. The Bible, like nearly every religion, says there is life after death. Shakespeare's quote is this:

"There are more things in Heaven and earth Horatio, than are dreamt of in your philosophy".

I always took that line to mean that there may be energies, entities, spirits, guardian angels, you know…the kinds of things that go beyond what we can see and touch or even understand.

I just want to mention the most recent of those coincidences or maybe it was just bad timing on my part. In June of this year, I decided to write a fan letter. It was the first fan letter I've ever written to anybody. It took me nearly two weeks to get it worded just right. I wanted the recipient to understand why I was writing it to them. I didn't ask for a signed photograph or anything like that. The letter was just to say *thank you* for having influenced me and how that influence had affected my life.

The letter was addressed to the eighty-nine-year-old Ms. Linda Cristal, the actress from "The High Chaparral". I mailed that letter to her on the morning of June 26th, 2020. A few days later, I found out that on the evening of June 27th Ms. Cristal had passed away in her sleep. Whether it was coincidence or bad timing, she didn't receive my letter.

Until a year and a half ago, there were only a handful of people who knew about just bits and pieces of the events that I'm about to tell you. As of today, there are about a dozen who know those bits and pieces and only three who know what I've written here. It's the story of a very remarkable woman who, for me, became the benchmark for all the women who came after her.

Acknowledgements

I'd like to thank my first wife, Anna Lee, for being a wonderful wife and very good mother to our children. Her love for me was unwavering. I want to apologize to her for not being the husband to her that I should have been, that I could have been. I loved her very much, but my past was still very fresh in my mind and in my heart when we met and married. I'd hoped my past wouldn't affect our marriage, but I wasn't strong enough to follow through. Our end was unfortunate, but understandable. I'm deeply sorry for my transgressions during our relationship. She deserved much better than me.

As well, I'd like to thank my second wife, Diane, for saving me from myself at a point in my life that had become a very dark time for me. We had many good years together and, for the most part, it was the most wonderful time in my life. She allowed me to be at peace with myself and to be happy to greet each new day with a smile and a reason for living. However, I have no apologies for her. I gave to her of myself in a way that I didn't think would ever be possible. By my choice, I sacrificed everything I knew before I'd met her…my family, my friends, and especially my children. I wasn't there for them as they grew up as they needed me close by for them. In the end, walking away from her was not what I wanted…it was what she wanted, and it was the last sacrifice that I would make for her.

I want to thank Kay. This is one fantastic woman with a good heart. We forged a friendship, just a friendship and nothing more. Not that I didn't try to take it beyond that when I was available to do so! She helped me through a very tough time in my life, when I wouldn't and couldn't turn to friends or family. I've referred to her as both an "Angel on my shoulder" and my "Happy Pill." In life, there are coincidences, then…there are statistical improbabilities. When it comes to Kay, the statistical improbabilities are astronomical.

And a very big thank you to my friends Ray and Stu who have been there for me over the last few years and taken me under their wings. Their friendship has been a saving grace for me.

Finally, there is one more person to thank that I have to wait to divulge. You, the reader, will eventually understand why.

Chapter One

Monday - March 1st, 1976

It's a cold damp dark evening in my hometown just north of New York City. The weather this time of year only rivals November in the NYC area. You just don't want to be out after dark. The cold and dampness goes right through you to your bones.

I was in college and was still living with my parents and younger brother. I worked a few days a week at the local supermarket stocking shelves, Tuesday and Thursday evenings and all day Saturday.

After dinner, my cousin James called to ask me if I would join him Wednesday evening for a couple of hours. He was dating a girl in a neighboring town, and she had a girlfriend. The girls wanted to go for drinks for a couple of hours at a local bar. Wednesday was ladies' night and the girls could drink for free from 7 to 9 pm.

I told him I didn't really want to go out especially on a blind date. I asked him if he could tell me anything about her. He said that he didn't know anything since he'd never met her. He didn't even know her name.

He said, "Mike, it isn't really a date. It's just so there will be four of us."

I declined again.

The next night he called again, and again I initially refused. Then I began to feel bad. James was my cousin, but we were very close, more like brothers, so I finally agreed to join him Wednesday evening. I had no way of knowing how my life was about to change.

Wednesday - March 3rd

My cousin picked me up at about 6:30 pm. It was only a 15-minute drive to his girlfriend's place. She was ready, and we headed over to her friend's apartment a few blocks away. We found a parking space, entered the apartment building, and took the elevator to the third floor. We knocked and she cracked the door open slightly and spoke to my cousin's date. She was still getting dressed so we waited a few seconds so she could get back to her bedroom, then we went in and waited in the living room.

At this point, I still hadn't seen her yet, but there was a photo of two young kids, maybe about 5 and 8 years old on the wall. So, I assumed she was divorced and, of course, a bit older than me.

James and his girlfriend were sitting nearer the hallway on the couch. I was sitting toward the back of the room on a chair. A few minutes later, she walked into the hallway and under the large arched entry of the living room.

I'm glad I was sitting down.

With just the sight of her, I thought. it's her…Victoria Cannon. Oh, my God!

Then, she began to speak…with a Spanish accent!

No, it was not the actress, Linda Cristal, but as they say in horseshoes and hand grenades—close was good enough! I couldn't take my eyes off her.

She was about five feet tall, beautiful, slender, with long black hair down to the middle of her back, and her accent was the icing on the cake. We were finally introduced. She said her name was— and I'll write this the way she pronounced it with her Spanish accent—*Sorina*. I asked her if she could spell that for me, and she said *Z-o-r-i-n-a*.

I said, "Oh, Zorina."

She responded once again, "Yes, *Sorina*," with her Spanish accent.

I smiled and said, "It's very nice to meet you."

We got in James' car and headed over to Eddie's Bar & Grill, where we found an open table for four. I was not exactly a worldly guy at the age of twenty. The gift of gab was not my forte. For the next two hours, I was able to talk with her in a way that I'd never been able to do before with a girl. It was so easy.

Maybe in my younger years, having to listen to grown-ups was finally going to pay off for me. Maybe I was meant to be with someone a bit older than me, someone a bit more mature. We kept talking, and we were having a nice time.

Zorina was so beautiful and kind. Her smile was genuine, yet alluring. I kept thinking, "ask her out", but I felt she would just kindly say *no*, especially since she had mentioned that she was twenty-seven and dating someone. I mean, what could she want with a college guy who worked part time in a grocery store?

I mentioned to her that I already had plans to visit Connie, who I had dated from college the year before. I explained that Connie and I weren't very serious, but we did like each other. Zorina had an older guy who I supposed had a decent full-time job and who was ready to take on a girlfriend with two kids. While she was twenty-seven, she looked no more than about twenty-one.

I didn't ask her to go out. I just couldn't pull the trigger. She was getting a ride home from another friend of hers who was at the bar. Finally, before she left, she came back over to our table and said, "I'm leaving now. It was nice to meet you."

Once again, I was busting up inside to ask her out, but I still didn't do it.

Then, she said, "Would you like to go out sometime?"

I said, "Yes, I would really like that."

She wrote her phone number on a napkin and handed it to me. We said goodnight, and I told her I'd call her tomorrow.

I was flying high. The girl of my dreams just asked me to go out with her. If she hadn't asked me out, I may have never seen her again.

On Thursday evening, I called her. We spoke for a couple of minutes, and I asked her if she was available Friday evening to see a movie. She said *yes*, and I told her I'd pick her up around 6:00. I didn't give her any other details, but I had big plans. Where would any twenty-year old guy with a full-sized Chevy take an older, beautiful, divorced woman who asked him to go out, but to see a movie at a drive-in? So, that was my master plan…along with a six-pack of beer, of course!

Friday - March 5th
(Our first date; we always considered that to be our anniversary)

Friday night, I headed over to pick her up. An early March evening at a drive-in in NY could get pretty chilly. We were both dressed in jeans, and I told her where we were going, so she made sure she wore a warm coat. Her kids were at a neighbor's apartment, and she needed to be home by 10:00. I figured that timeline was very workable. We drove about twenty minutes north to the drive-in. It was a double-feature, and I have no recollection of what the two movies were, but then again, they weren't the point of the date as far as I was concerned.

We got there, pulled in, paid the entry fee, and found a parking space. It was already getting dark and the temperature began dropping. We were watching the movie a bit, talking a bit, and trying to stay warm.

I really liked just looking at her. She had a classic beauty that didn't require much, if any, makeup. I offered her a beer, and she accepted. She only had that one beer that evening.

Cold beer on a cold night…so I ran the car a few times over the next couple of hours to run the heater. We talked and watched some of the movie. While we were in conversation, I was watching every nuance of her facial expressions and how her hair fell on her shoulders. She was mesmerizing to me.

Finally, I was ready to make my move. It was nothing crazy. I wasn't the kind of guy to take advantage of a girl. It had to be a mutual thing, and I suppose that's why I had dated so few girls up to that point in my life and hadn't really gotten anywhere with them.

I had a bench style seat in the front, so I leaned over and tried to kiss her. She just kept watching the movie and didn't respond at all. She didn't turn toward me. She didn't say anything, but she didn't turn away either. So, I ended up kissing her on the left side of her lips.

It was a bit awkward, and I wondered why she wasn't a bit more "involved" in at least wanting to make out a little. I went back to watching the movie, and we talked some more. I can't remember any of the conversation that evening, but I do remember trying to get a kiss at least two more times.

I got the same results, although the final time I tried it, I did slide over toward her on the seat so I could have a better angle at a frontal attack, and hopefully catch a bigger portion of her lips, but she just kept watching the movie and didn't respond at all. Again, she didn't turn toward me. She didn't say anything, but she didn't turn away either.

At that point, I gracefully acknowledged to myself that the evening probably wasn't going to end the way I had planned. We made it through the first movie, and we were having a nice time just talking like the night we first met a couple of days before. There was some kind of chemistry between us that went beyond the physical. She made me feel good, and I hoped I made her feel the same way. It was something I'd never felt before.

It was after 9'oclock at this point, and the second movie was just getting started. She had to be home by 10, and it was getting colder outside by the minute, so I asked her if she wanted to head for home.

She said, "Yes, it's getting a bit late."

So, we headed back to her place. I parked and walked her to her door. We said goodnight, and I leaned over and gave her a kiss on the cheek. She didn't kiss me back, but I was okay with that. I told her I would call her over the weekend and said maybe we could get together again soon. She seemed to like that idea. All I knew was this—Zorina was a hottie with a Spanish accent, and I liked her. We seemed to be getting along very well like we had known each other for a long time. I was very upbeat about how things went that evening, even though it didn't turn out the way I had hoped it would.

I'm going to let you in on a secret that I hadn't yet realized. The evening had gone the way *she* had planned it, and I didn't understand that for a couple of more weeks. I'll explain that soon enough.

I didn't want to seem over anxious so I called her on Sunday. We spoke for a bit, and I asked her if we could get together on Monday or Tuesday afternoon. I was hoping she'd say Monday, since I had a couple of classes on Tuesday morning, and I had to go to work at 5'oclock. I think maybe she didn't want to seem over anxious either so she said Tuesday afternoon would be good. She wasn't working at this point in time. Her kids were in school, and my schedule allowed me to be free days or evenings, depending on the day.

I went over to her place at about noon on Tuesday. We talked for a while, and things got a bit romantic with just some kissing and heavy petting. Then, she asked if she could make love to me. That's how she worded it. So, what's a twenty-year old horn dog like me supposed to do except say, "Okay."

Now, listen up. Did you read the title of this memoir? If you want to read a detailed smut book, this ain't that kind of story! All I will say is that it was a very enlightening and pleasurable experience. We began to see each other nearly every day after that, and things progressed in our relationship in a very positive way.

There was still the issue of the guy she had been dating. They had been frequenting each other's company for over a year. A few days later, I was at her apartment. There was a knock on the door. It was her boyfriend calling her name, and he wasn't giving up. Fortunately, she had never given him a key.

That door was the only way in and out of that apartment. Well, except for a small window over the kitchen sink that led to the fire escape, which went to the roof where there was an access door to take the stairs down and out of the building.

Here's a major admission on my part—I was and still am deathly afraid of heights. She lived on the third floor, and it was a five-story building. Before I left, I asked her to call me after he left, since she planned on letting him in. That window was my only way out, so I took a deep breath, gave her a kiss, climbed over the kitchen sink, and went on my way.

When I got down to the street, he was down there pacing back and forth. I knew it was him, since she had previously shown me a photo of them together. As I walked by him, I glanced over. He was headed back into the building. I made my way to my car and took off for home.

When she called, she told me she jumped in the shower after I left, so when she opened the door for him, she was dripping wet and he didn't suspect anything. She was in a relationship with him, but she had told me she was having second thoughts about it. I wasn't sure which of us she would choose. Eventually, I found out that he'd been both verbally and physically abusive to her. I had no idea that she was dealing with that type of treatment by this guy. We'd only been seeing each other for a couple of weeks, but I was falling in love with her. I didn't understand that at that point in time, since I had nothing to compare it to.

A couple of days later, she called me at home. She said she wanted to see me. She had something important to talk to me about. I said *okay*, and I jumped in my car. I just knew it was about her making a choice between me and the other guy. I felt that if she had decided to stay with me and break up with him, she would have told me that on the phone. I was a wreck on the drive over to her place. I had tears rolling down my face the entire fifteen minutes. This wonderful woman that I'd met was going to cut me loose. I'd never felt this way about anything or anyone before in my life, and now it was going to end.

Before I went up to her apartment, I had to get myself together. I hoped she wouldn't be able to tell that I'd been crying. When I went in, she just said, "Hi", and we spoke for a minute.

I was trying to act normal, but I was very edgy. She took my hand and led me over to the couch, and we sat down. She looked at me with her piercing dark eyes and said, "Mike, I have something I need to tell you."

I just thought, here it comes. She's going to stay with her boyfriend while being kind and gracious to me as to try to not hurt my feelings.

Zorina then said she'd come to a decision about me and him. I tried desperately to stay calm. Then she said, "I've decided to stop seeing him. I want to date only you."

I sat there for a few seconds and was processing what I'd just heard her say to me. Then I smiled, and kissed her, and admitted to her that I'd cried all the way over to her place because I thought she was going to end our relationship. She told me she cared about me very much, and she was happier than she'd been in a very long time. I told her that I'd never felt this way before.

It was the beginning of something very beautiful. It was also the beginning of something that neither of us was prepared for. We were both so emotionally involved, neither of us had thought things through. We were living for today, and today was fantastic, and tomorrow and the day after that would have to be the same way. And it was like that for quite a while.

We were together now on a daily basis. For me, it was a realization that I had only been a half a person prior to meeting her. Now I felt whole. She complemented me and I her as well. We were both the missing pieces of the puzzle for each other.

One afternoon, we were at her place and talking about how we first met. I told her how I hadn't even wanted to go out that night and how I wanted to ask her out, but I felt that she would say *no*. Then I asked her why she asked me out.

Remember earlier when I made a point of telling you about myself? Well, this is why. Her response seemed unusual to me.

She said, and I quote this because I'll never forget it, "I asked you out because you remind me of Richie Cunningham."

For those of you who are too young to know the reference, search for it on the internet. I immediately thought, I don't really look like Richie.

She didn't elaborate on her response. It took me a while to understand that she was comparing the type of guy I was to the TV character. It was actually a very kind and fairly accurate comment on her part. That comparison also ties in to our first date at the drive-in.

I eventually realized that her lack of response to my advances was a test for me. She was trying to find out if I was, in fact, the type of guy she thought I might be, if I actually was who she expected me to be. As it turned out, I was Richie in the flesh, and I passed her test with flying colors.

It's a funny thing. I was looking for a girl like Victoria Cannon, and she was looking for a guy like Richie Cunningham. We both got our wishes.

One last thing about that. Richie's Mom's name in the TV show was Marion. My Mom's name is Marion. Just another one of those silly coincidences.

Zorina and I had been seeing each other for about three weeks now. It was late March, and I'd learned a lot about her in that time. Her son and daughter were really good kids. The photo that I'd seen hanging in her apartment the first night I met her was actually a few years old. She'd had another daughter that unfortunately passed away about five years earlier at the age of five. It seems that daughter, Gigi, had passed away after getting vaccinations for school, although her death was listed as caused by "heart failure".

Her son Luca was now eleven and her daughter Jeannette was just turning eight years old. Here's an odd coincidence that I was always amazed by, although it's not really earth shattering by any means. My Godmother's name is Jeannette (my Mom's sister), and my Godfather's name was Luca (my Dad's best friend since they were teenagers). I mean, what were the odds that could happen?

Zorina had a birthday party for her daughter, and it was the first and only time I met her ex-husband. He seemed like a really nice guy. Zorina had been born and raised in a small town on the western end of Puerto Rico, came to the States in about 1963, and learned English after she moved here. At that point in time, I didn't know the name of her hometown. Culturally, she was very different than American girls, and I really liked that.

One night at Eddie's Bar, we were hanging out with some of her friends. At some point, she said a Spanish word that I took notice of. The word was *munequita*, pronounced *moonyakeeta*. I asked her what it meant.

She said it kind of meant like "baby doll" or "little doll". She explained that a guy might call his girlfriend or wife *munequita* as a loving endearing term.

I liked it. I liked it a lot, and I would call her that every once in a while, just to let her know how special she was to me. Many years later that term was used in a song by Rob Thomas and Carlos Santana. I was with some friends one evening, and that song was on the radio. Someone asked what's that word, and they wondered what it meant.

I blurted out, "That's *munequita*, and it means like baby doll. A guy would call his girl that nickname."

They all looked at me like I had three heads. I got responses from them of "really?" and "how do you know that?" My answer was concise and straight to the point.

I said, "Because I had one of those."

I don't think they were sure if they should believe me or not, or if I was serious about what I'd just said, but they didn't pursue the topic any further. I just sat there and smiled with a shit-eating grin on my face.

As different as Zorina and I were we had common interests, especially when it came to music. Disco was still getting a foot hold, and we both enjoyed it, but we both also really liked the black groups from the late '50's through the early '70's.

My best friend Big Sal was a bouncer by night and a truck driver by day. He was pushing 6'4" and weighed in at about nearly 300lbs. Sal was a wanna be comedian. He was always telling jokes and funny stories and made people laugh. He eventually became a standup comic, and many years later did a movie with actors Chazz Palmentieri and Robert Davi.

He was working at a club on the edge of the north Bronx at 238th Street and White Plains Road, just about a mile from where I lived. He told me the singing group The Drifters were coming to perform there for a one-night show. They'd had a string of huge hits from the early 50's through the mid 60's like "On Broadway", "Under the Boardwalk", "Up on the Roof", "Some Kind of Wonderful", and "This Magic Moment".

I asked Zorina if she'd like to go to the show, and she was all about it. She got to meet Sal for the first time, and The Drifters put on a great show with at least fifteen of their biggest hits. It was a fun night, and we had a great time.

About a week later, I thought maybe a bit of a more upscale place would be nice to have drinks and maybe a bite to eat, so I decided to take her to Tarrytown to the Hilton Hotel. I went to pick her up at her place. She was still getting dressed when I arrived, so I was waiting for her in the living room. She was in the bedroom and asked me to help her get her dress zipped up. She hadn't put it on yet. I never watched a girl getting dressed before, at least not with the light on. She stepped into the dress, pulled it up from the floor, and put her arms through the sleeves. Then she asked, "Can you zip me up?"

I zipped her dress up, then she turned toward me and kissed me. I was just going with the flow. This was a totally new experience for me, and you know what? I really liked it!

Before we headed up to the Hilton, I took her to where I lived with my parents and brother, Dominick. It was after 5'oclock, and I'd hoped she could meet everyone. My brother was out some-where, and my dad wasn't home yet, but my mom was there.

They met, and my mom was so gracious. Zorina was a real peo-ple person so her and my mom were yacking away for about thirty minutes. My Dad and brother never did get home in time so we headed out. We got to the Hilton about thirty minutes later.

What I remember about the Hilton was the big stone fireplace in the bar area. There were small, round, low tables and comfy chairs to get cozy in and have a cocktail. She looked so beautiful that night. I remember us looking at each other at one point, and it was the first time that I thought to myself that I was in love with her, and I had no doubts about it. From the look in her eyes, I think she felt the same way.

I kept one of the drink stirrers from that evening as a memento, and I still have it. It's a white stirrer about six inches long with the letter "H" on top.

We didn't stay there for the night. Working twelve hours a week part-time at the supermarket at $2.30 an hour wasn't very lucrative. Yeah, that's right. Minimum wage was $2.30 an hour, so on about $25 a week, I had to put gas in my car and take my girlfriend out a couple of nights a week. Zorina was very understanding about that, so we made it work.

We became inseparable. We were together now every day at some point. She always had people over at her apartment. Usually, they were neighbors from the building. We were both so considerate and respectful of each other, and we were always trying to make sure the other one was comfortable, no matter what situation we might be in.

Sometimes when I had a class or two, she would take the ride to the college with me. I'd go to class for an hour or two, while she stayed in the car. Then we'd head back to her place. We were very compatible in a variety of ways, and our days were spent enjoying each other's company.

Wink. Wink.

Chapter Two

April 1976

In early April, I was at her place, and she told me she had an album that she wanted me to listen to. It was Barry White's Stone Gon' album. At her direction, I had to listen to the songs in a certain order that she had circled and numbered on the back cover. The order was 3,1,4,5, and 2 was last. Barry could really set the mood for a couple.

Her dedicating this album to me was the first moment I began to realize how passionate she was about our relationship. Although it's so scratched that it's unplayable, I do still have that album.

Zorina instilled a confidence in me that I'd never had before with a girl. She told me straight out that I was a handsome guy, I was good and kind, and that any girl would want to have a guy like me. I do admit that no girl had ever said anything even remotely similar to that about me, so who was I to argue with her assessment of me? A few days later on April 8th she gave me a card and wrote something in it that was from the heart and very beautiful.

To Mike,

I may not always understand you, but until there was you each day that passed was like the day before. But now the world is beautiful – the earth – the sky – everything around just shines. But with that beautiful smile! How could it not happen. Thank you for being so nice. I am going to miss you when you go on your trip.

Love always, Z

We had only been dating about a month, but things were moving very quickly with us. I had a ring that I wore most of the time on my left pinkie finger that had my initials engraved on it. It had been given to me on my Catholic Confirmation when I was about eight years old by my grandparents. Z wanted me to give her that ring to wear.

Instead, I gave her another ring to wear that I wore once in a while on my pinkie finger. It was just a gold-plated ring with a blue oval-shaped stone in it, and it fit her ring finger perfectly. She knew it wasn't expensive, but it was the thought behind it. I still have that ring. Years later, I would end up giving her the ring with my initials engraved on it that she originally requested from me.

April was a busy month for us. Zorina wanted to go to church on Palm Sunday, so I took her to the church I had attended since I was a kid. Easter always seemed to be her favorite religious holiday. In a card that she gave me dated April 15th, 1976 she wrote:

To my Mike,

No moments or hours like moments of ours!
Happy Easter to someone very special.
P.S. Together with your family.
Love, Z

We went to a party that her brother, Jose, was having one evening at his apartment right off the Grand Concourse in the Bronx, just north of Yankee Stadium. It was a fun time. He was a very friendly, funny guy and really made me feel welcome. That month we also visited her mom one day in the south Bronx, Hunts Point to be exact.

For a green kid from the suburbs, going to the south Bronx was a bit of a culture shock. Her Mom was very nice and tried to make sure I was comfortable. She didn't speak much English, so they spoke in Spanish most of the time.

Her Mom lived on the second floor of an apartment building, and we were able to park on the street right under her windows. Across the street from her building, there were blocks of empty lots where there had been other apartment buildings at some point in time, but now there was just some brick rubble over that whole area. Every fifteen minutes or so, I would go to the window and make sure my car was still there and the tires were still on it. You can call me paranoid if you'd like, but this was a rough neighborhood. We were there about ninety minutes and headed back north much to my delight!

One evening, we caught a movie in Bronxville and started back to her place. Well, we couldn't wait the twenty minutes to get there. We were both sort of worked up a bit for some reason. I knew about a wooded, semi-hidden dirt road right off the Bronx River Parkway exit to Bronxville, so we pulled in there.

It was a cool damp night, so the windows fogged up pretty quick once we parked. Five minutes later, we were about half dressed in the back seat and then came a knock on the car window. It was a police officer asking if everything was alright, and we both responded *yes*. Then, he let us know that we needed to leave the area pronto. We were both very appreciative that we didn't have to exit the car while we were parked there. We laughed about it all the way to her place.

We were going out maybe one night a week to the clubs and meeting up with my brother Dom, my cousin James, as well as my friends once in a while. At that time in New York, the drinking age was eighteen. Whenever we went to the clubs, she would get carded. As I said earlier, she was twenty-seven, but she didn't look that old at all.

I played softball with the guys from a local disco that I frequented, where Big Sal was a bouncer. Sal worked at a couple of
different clubs. Boy Boy's was a neighborhood place and everybody knew everybody there. On Sunday mornings, we'd have a
couple of softball games against either another bar or one of the
local taxi-cab companies. Zorina loved to attend the games, and
I liked to show off for her. She only lived a couple of miles from
where we played, so it was really convenient for her to join me,
and I was glad to have her there.

Sometime in late April, she brought up the subject of marriage.
She said she was very much in love with me, and I told her I was
very much in love with her, as well. She said it didn't have to be a
fancy wedding, that we could just go to the Justice of the Peace at
City Hall and get it done.

I told her I wasn't ready for marriage. I was still in college, and
I didn't even have a halfway decent job making any kind of money. Besides, we'd only been dating for less than two months. She
didn't care. She loved me for me and for no other reason.

My family didn't have money. My Dad was a working guy,
making wages, and my mom was a housewife. We lived in a rented
apartment. I think Zorina was, to some extent, concerned about my
planned trip to see Connie over Memorial Day.

Zorina came from a poor background in a small town in Puerto Rico. She didn't have much even at this point in time, and she
knew I couldn't provide for her financially. She made due with
what she had. She was old school, and more than that, she was old
world. That was her through and through.

For her, she was about the "man", his needs and wants, and she
would totally support him and back him up. It was a cultural thing
due to her upbringing. She didn't know any other way. As I said
earlier, she found in me the type of guy she had dreamt about. A
clean cut, decent type that treated her with respect and kindness,
and we just clicked from day-one with a chemistry between us that
to this day I look back on as an amazing rarity.

Her life up to that point had limited her options in men. Her ex was, as far as I've ever known, a nice and decent guy. At some point they had a falling out at least five years before I met her. I never delved into what happened there, but they seemed to be on good terms.

Once I explained to her why I wouldn't agree to getting married, she understood and seemed okay with it. I think she just didn't want anything to go wrong with us. Many times, she'd tell me how fortunate we were to have the relationship we had, how rare and special it was.

She'd experienced life already. For me, I couldn't completely grasp much of that. I was too young and inexperienced to fully appreciate what she already knew about life. All I knew was I had a beautiful, caring, giving, trusting and trustworthy woman who loved me very much and would do anything for me, and I mean *anything*. That was the first of five times that the subject of marriage would come up between us over an eleven-year period.

She sent me another card in early April with some more personal sentiments that she wrote in it. Here is just a portion of it:

Dedicated to Mike,

Love begins with a feeling of security. You are warm with a sense of her nearness even when she is away. Time does not separate you. You need her near, but near or away you know she is yours and you can't wait. Love has an element of sexual excitement. If you are honest, you will discover how beautiful you're able to enjoy one another. You know it will end in intimacy.

Love, Zorina

We were a couple, and nothing could separate us. We were extremely happy together, and we would do anything for each other. Neither of us was demanding, or pushy, or selfish. I spent my first full night with Zorina sometime in late April or early May. We were on cruise control, and life was good. Many years later, I reflected back on that time in a poem I wrote:

Young I was
Free I was
Gentle, so gentle
And in love I was

A walk in the park
A kiss after dark
Goodnight, oh goodnight
And in love I was

Smelling the flowers
Long walks for hours
Through the leaves
And in love I was

A simpler time
When you were mine
So simple, so gentle
And in love I was

Zorina and I were just as happy as two people could possibly be.
I was going to school, hanging out with friends, playing softball,
and spending lots of time with her. The beaches weren't open yet,
but we were looking forward to the sun, sand, and ocean by June. I
was planning my trip to see Connie for a few days at the end of the
month with a buddy of mine. Memorial Day was the last day of the
month that year, so I was planning the trip for the 28th – 31st. Connie knew about Zorina from the letters we were sending each other.
I don't think either me or Connie thought anything would come of
my visit to see her. We dated in college, but we weren't really that
romantically involved.

In early May, my dad wanted to have a conversation with me.
He wasn't exactly the *Ward Cleaver* type, but he always had my
best interests at heart. He also wasn't the type to want to debate or
discuss things. Pretty much what he said was the way it was going
to be. The subject of the talk was Zorina.

I think my recent staying out all night with her got his attention.
He asked me about her, so I told him. He hadn't met her, so I gave
him a rundown on her age, kids, and being divorced. None of that
set well with him. He advised me that I should meet someone my
own age or younger, who didn't have kids, and had never been
married.

He said, "You're a young guy. You haven't finished college yet,
and you're not making any kind of money."

He wanted me to stop seeing her, and he was very adamant
about it. I didn't argue with him. It would just have made things
worse. He knew I was planning to visit Connie in a few weeks,
so I was hoping that he might see that as me not really being that
serious about Zorina.

I saw her the next day and told her what my Dad had said to me. She was already concerned about our relationship due to my upcoming trip, and now my dad was putting pressure on me. I didn't plan any more overnights at her place. I was hoping things would just calm down a bit. I was very much in love with her, but I did still have feelings for Connie as well. I'd reached that point in my life where I had to start making my own decisions, even though I couldn't go out on my own due to finances. In late June, I would start a summer job making $100 a week, as well as working at the supermarket, but the summer job would only last through September.

Zorina and I kept seeing each other, but it was an emotional time for both of us. She felt that my Dad didn't like her, but I tried to explain that it was just our situation and not anything on a personal level about her that was his concern. A couple of weeks later, I was at her place and was going to head home for dinner. I got in my car, and it wouldn't start. The battery was dead.

I tried to call my cousin and my brother for a jump start but couldn't reach either one of them. I only had one option…call Dad. He arrived about thirty minutes later, and we hooked the cables up and got it going.

Zorina was sitting on the steps to her apartment building about a hundred feet away. She didn't come over, and my dad didn't ask to meet her. It was the one and only time he ever saw her. He finished up and headed home.

I said goodnight to her and headed home for dinner. That evening he told me again that he wanted me to end the relationship. I was trying to find the courage to defy my dad's wishes, while I was agonizing over the possibility of not having her in my life. If there ever was getting caught between a rock and a hard place this was it. Thirty-two years later he would make a comment about that day.

Z and I were still cruising along. We were very much in love, but I had that trip coming up. I know, I know. I was twenty years old, and I had this twenty-seven-year-old hottie, so I was a horn dog being sexually satisfied.

Wrong. Wrong. Wrong!

As I stated earlier, the physical part of things was good (okay, it was great), but there was a connection on an emotional and spiritual level that was there as well. Why do you think I'm sitting here writing this nearly forty-five years after the fact?

Sex is just sex, but real love and a bond between two people doesn't happen every day. As things progress, you'll better understand the depth of our relationship. A *bond*…I don't use that term lightly. Bonds are usually formed under very difficult situations. We formed a bond. It's still here today as it will be forever.

At that point, I didn't understand what Z was going through emotionally. I knew she was very much in love with me, but I didn't really understand what that entailed. Again, I had nothing to compare it to. I wasn't able to put myself in her situation. She was so kind and understanding during this period. This was a proud and strong woman who could handle any situation, but when it came to our relationship, there was a weakness in her for me and for us. In effect, I was her Achilles heel.

We kept things going through the rest of May, but the uncertainty of my trip and my Dad's wishes was weighing heavily on both of us. We still had each other to lean on, but it was very hard for me to imagine not having her in my life, not having her by my side.

I'd seen Zorina the night before my trip, and she was so understanding, but I could see the hurt in her eyes. Our relationship hung in the balance, and I was the one making the decisions, while she continued to try to explain to me how special and rare things were between us. I told her I loved her, and she said she loved me, and was going to miss me very much. I headed home for a good night's sleep. I had an all-day drive ahead of me on Friday.

The day had come to take the trip to see Connie. Jerry, a buddy of mine, traveled with me. It was a long drive, and we had to stop for gas twice. We finally arrived, and Connie and her roommate, Donna, greeted us.

They shared a rented trailer near the college campus they attended. It was a roof over their heads and quite comfy, but it was a no frills place as you'd expect a couple of college students to have. Jerry and I stayed in the living room and slept on the couch and a chair, while the girls stayed in their bedrooms.

We all did some things together on Saturday. On Sunday, Jerry and Donna took off for a few hours to give Connie and me some alone time. Connie and I liked each other a lot, but we weren't in love with each other. Even though we had been writing to each other over the past year, it was nice to spend time together.

She already knew about Zorina, and I filled her in on what was recently going on with us. Connie didn't take sides regarding my situation. She could tell that I wasn't sure what I should do. My life was at a crossroads, and I was the only one who could decide what direction to go in. Our time that afternoon was nice and fun.

Jerry and Donna returned, and we all had dinner. On Monday morning, Connie and I said our goodbyes, and Jerry and I started our trip back to New York. The good, decent guy who tried to do right by everybody was about to make a decision that he hoped would be the right thing to do, but what Zorina had originally found so appealing about me being like "Richie" was about to become a nightmare for both of us.

June 1976

I did a little research on memoirs before I started this just to try to get a handle on what was involved, and some of the rules that I should be aware of. At one point, it was mentioned that sometimes when writing a memoir, the memories and the reliving of certain moments can be emotionally overwhelming.

I've had a couple of those moments so far, but what I'm about to cover in June is going to be the toughest to put on paper. When I've spoken to friends about the events of this month, I've had to stop and take a deep breath from time to time because I can hardly get the words out. After nearly forty-five years, I still experience a very deep emotional upheaval when I think about the things that happened.

Chapter Three

June 1ˢᵗ

I got together with Z at Eddy's Bar that evening. It was so good to be back and see her, and she was glad to see me too. She had an Eddie's Bar matchbook, and she wrote a one line note to me in it. It said, *I missed you while you were gone.*

It was a silly little thing, but it meant so much to me. As I stated in the beginning, I'm a sentimental fool and a hopeless romantic. The matchbook is just another one of those little things that I kept, and I still have it.

Along with the matchbook, she gave me a 45rpm record, "Right Back Where We Started From." She was upbeat that my trip away from her was done, and we could pick up where we left off, and get our relationship moving again. You guessed it. Yes, I still have that original 45 she gave me.

Then, in a card dated June 2ⁿᵈ she wrote this, sensing I was not quite the same as I had been before I left to visit Connie:

Dear Mike,

I do mean I hope with all my heart all your dreams come true. Because I will never want to see you hurt. Remember the day I said I Love You, well - I also said that it didn't mean that you never had to go…it meant I wish you never had to.

Love, Zorina

Everything could be so wonderful and amazing, but I did have doubts about staying together. Maybe my dad was right, and I should find a girl who was closer to my age and didn't have a family already. I didn't have a full-time job yet, and I had another year of college to go. Maybe Zorina would be better off finding an older guy who was financially established and prepared to support her and her children.

Lots of maybes. My inner "Richie" was trying to look at the situation from a logical point of view, but love isn't logical. It's pure emotion, and I was fighting with that in my head and in my heart. I loved her so much, and I couldn't imagine not having her in my life, but maybe it was the right thing to do.

By the weekend. I told Zorina that I thought we should stop seeing each other. She was very deeply hurt by the prospect of us no longer being together. Once again, she tried to explain to me how special and how rare our love was. She never got angry, she never yelled, and she never even got an attitude about it. What did happen was she became frustrated that she couldn't make me understand what we had with each other.

During this time, she told me she might be pregnant. I told her that having a child was not an option, if she actually was pregnant. She said if she did have our baby, that she wouldn't expect anything from me, that she would have it and be responsible for it.

Over the next two weeks, we saw each other just a couple of days a week, and her frustration turned into anxiety and then depression. There was a helplessness about her, and no matter what she tried to do or say, it was of no use.

I didn't like being apart from her either, but I hoped in the long run, somehow, we'd both be better off. She'd exhausted all of her options, and I could see how she was having an internal battle to find a way to stop what was happening or accept how things were going to be. And still, on my birthday she gave me a card that said this:

God bless you today and every day of your life, for as long as you live. I hope that all your dreams come true.

Love, Zorina

Six Days in June

Day 1 - June 21ˢᵗ

Zorina called me and asked me to come over to her place. A girlfriend of hers was there with her for moral support. Her kids weren't there. I think they'd just finished the school year and may have been with her ex-husband. Z was very physically exhausted from loss of sleep due to what was happening with us. I hated to see her like that. She was a woman that only gave of herself and asked for very little to nothing in return.

She gave me a small 2 by 3 inch card that came with a necklace with two hearts joined side by side that she got at a card shop. She dated it June 22ⁿᵈ because she had planned on mailing it to me the next day. As I'm writing this, I'm looking at that card. I still have the necklace as well as the envelope that has a stamp on it with no postmark.

In the card she wrote:

I'm sorry…let's forgive and forget. Please forgive me you know I would never do anything to hurt you. Please don't do it to me.   - Z

She was apologizing to me, but she hadn't done anything wrong. I never told her that she did anything wrong or bad because she hadn't. She'd been everything to me. I was never upset or angry with her at all at any time in our relationship. I loved her, and I had been so kind and good to her, and she'd made me so happy.

Like I said, she had exhausted all of her options. I guess, this was all she felt she could do or say to keep us together even though what she was doing didn't make any sense. I knew she was on edge. She wasn't thinking clearly. Her demeanor was that of being defeated, there were tears in her eyes.

I told her we'd talk about things, but that she needed to get some rest. I pulled her girlfriend aside and told her whatever you do please don't leave her alone, and she agreed. I said goodnight to Z and headed home.

I was very upset and very nervous about her state of mind. I could never forgive myself if anything happened to her. What I didn't understand was that Zorina had just given me that card and necklace as a last resort. My telling her she needed rest and pushing a resolution out further was a "no" response to her. She decided to accept the way things were going to be, but with that acceptance things were about to go from bad to worse.

Day 2 - June 22nd

In the early afternoon hours of June 22nd, 1976 Zorina's breathing, heart, and pulse had stopped.

My car's rear brakes had been squealing for a couple of weeks, so I was scheduled to drop it off at the mechanic Tuesday morning. Both the repair shop and my summer job were about a half mile from where I lived. I dropped the car off in the morning and walked to work from there.

At noon, I walked home for lunch. Before I left to go back to work, I called Z. The phone rang a few times, and she picked it up. She was mumbling incoherently and not making any sense. I tried talking to her, but she dropped the phone and picked it back up. She was really out of it, and I knew what she'd done.

She'd taken an overdose of sleeping pills, but she was still half awake. I hung up, and I wanted to go over there, but I didn't have any transportation. I didn't want to wait for a cab either, since time could be a factor. I called the operator, told her Z's name, address, and apartment number, and that she had taken an overdose of sleeping pills. I stressed that Z was very incoherent. The operator took my name and number and said someone would call me back later. We hung up, and I headed back to work.

I was nervous and shaking as I walked back to work, and I was on edge all afternoon. I prayed that the police and the emergency personnel would get there right away. For whatever reason, the possibility of her dying didn't cross my mind since when I called her, she was still awake and able to answer the phone.

I got off work at 5:00 and went over to get my car. It was ready, and I drove home. I asked my mom if I'd had any phone calls, and she said no. A few minutes later, the phone rang. My mom answered it and said someone was calling for me.

I took the call on the phone in the other room. The caller identified himself as a police officer, who had been dispatched to the scene. I asked him if Zorina was alright, and he said she was in the ICU in a coma. He said the doctors only gave her a 50/50 chance of surviving. I was just trying to handle what he was telling me.

Then he said, "There's one other thing. Even if she does come out of the coma, she might not be the same as she was before."

I didn't understand what he was talking about, so I asked him to please explain. He said that when they arrived at her apartment they had to break the door down. She was on the floor. They checked her vital signs, and there was nothing. No heartbeat, no pulse, nothing. They had to use the electro shock machine three times to get her heart going. She was never conscious. He said they didn't know for how long her heart had stopped before they arrived, so her brain could have been deprived of oxygen long enough for her to be mentally and/or physically impaired, if she did wake up.

I thanked him and asked him what time visiting hours ended, and he said in about fifteen minutes. We hung up. I was numb. I told my Mom I had to go out for a while. I just had to leave our apartment for a while to get myself together.

There wasn't enough time to get to the hospital to see Z. I prayed to God to please don't let her die. Please let her wake up and be okay. I loved her so much. Everything had been so beautiful and wonderful with both of us since the night we first met, but the last couple of weeks had become a nightmare due to the decision I had made to stop seeing each other.

I didn't mean for any of this to happen. I'd hoped I was doing the right thing by ending the relationship even though it was tearing me apart as well. I was an emotional wreck. She might die, and if she did live, she might not be who she was anymore. To this day, I still feel the guilt of hurting someone so beautiful, so caring, so giving, and with so much love in them not only for me, but for everyone who came into contact with her.

Day 3 - June 23rd

On Wednesday, I went to the hospital. I was very anxious and emotionally distraught on the drive over there. The hospital was only a couple of miles from where Zorina lived. I pulled into the parking lot, parked, and began a slow run to the entrance. I asked the information desk where the ICU was located, and they said it was on the second floor. I didn't want to wait for the elevator, so I ran up the stairs.

The doorway to the second floor opened right up in front of the ICU. There were big glass windows that looked right into the ICU, and there were about six beds in the area. Zorina was the only patient in there. There were no other visitors there when I arrived.

I walked over to the desk where a nurse was sitting, and I asked her if I could go in to see Z. The nurse said no visitors were allowed in the ICU, that was hospital policy.

I looked at Zorina through the windows. I could see that she had tubes running into her mouth and nose. There were electrodes on her arms and chest, as well as a tube in her arm from an IV. My heart sank. She was in a coma, and I couldn't even be in the same room with her.

I was there looking at her for a few minutes, and I didn't know what else to do, so I turned toward the door and began to open it to go back down the stairs. I opened the door a few inches and stopped. All that went through my mind was that she could die, and I might never see her alive again, and if she did live, she might be handicapped. I let go of the door handle and turned back toward the nurse's station.

I asked the nurse again if I could go in to see her. The nurse said, "No, I'm sorry."

Then, hardly being able to get the words out, I said, "Can I please go in? She's here because of me."

The nurse saw how upset I was, and said, "Okay, but you can only go in for a few minutes."

I thanked her, went in, and stood alongside Zorina's bed. I stood there for a minute and just looked at her. Even in her condition she was so beautiful. I told her I loved her very much, and that I wanted her to get better, hoping that she might hear my voice and regain consciousness.

She just lay there breathing, hooked up to all those tubes and wires. I asked God to please, please let her live, and let her be okay like she was before. I knew that wasn't enough for me to say, so I decided to take it a step further.

I'd make a deal with God, and when you make a deal, you get something, and you give something. This was the deal.

"God, you let her live, and be okay like she was before, and you can take me. Take me in her place. All she did was love me. Please, take me instead of her."

And I meant it.

I said to Z that I'd be back the next day to see her, and that she needed to get better. I left the ICU room and thanked the nurse for letting me go in. I went back down the stairs to the reception area and into the parking lot. I was in tears as I headed to my car. As I was walking across the parking lot, a gray-haired priest was headed into the hospital. We made eye contact, and I stopped him.

I said "Father, can you please say a prayer for someone in the ICU? She's in a coma."

He said he would, and I told him Zorina's name. Her life was in God's hands, and I was hoping that the deal that I offered would be accepted. I got in my car and headed home.

At that point in time, I didn't know for sure if she had been pregnant or not when this all happened. The police officer I spoke to didn't mention it and neither did the nurse at the hospital when I went to see Zorina. Nearly eleven years later, I would ask her once again if she had been pregnant.

Day 4 - June 24th

I called the hospital late morning to see if there was any change in Zorina's condition. The nurse on the desk said she wasn't there anymore. A shock wave ran through me when she said that. I thought of the worst that could have happened. Then she said that Z had regained consciousness in the very early hours of Thursday morning. She said Zorina was able to answer questions, her motor skills were okay, and her mental state was determined to be fine. Z was then released a few hours later.

I thanked the nurse, hung up the phone, and then I thanked God. I don't know who that priest was that I spoke to in the parking lot the day before, but I thought he must have been in good standing with the Almighty.

I'd made a deal, and I was prepared to keep my end of the bargain.
Here's a tip. Don't try to make deals with God. He might fulfill
His end of a bargain, but He might not let you fulfill yours. He had
other plans for me that would take effect in early September.

One night, almost fourteen years later, I dreamt about Zorina.
I wrote two poems that were inspired by that dream and by the
events of those four days in June '76. Here they are:

The Dream

Saw you last night
Before I awoke
We talked and laughed
Like we used to

You were as I remember you
So young and carefree
So beautiful and so
Glad to be with me

All the things I've wanted
You wanted too
For us to be together
Together me and you

But even in my dream
The realities I faced
Still tormenting me
I still want a place

For us to go
So far away
So no one can hurt us
So we can love and play

The years have been
So good to me
But inside I'm tired
Longing to be free

Feelings lay dormant
Like flowers in the cold
Waiting for the spring
To free me from this hold

The Black Dream

Black dream of memories past
Black dream I wished wouldn't last
The rose should not wither
Take me, take me

The rose I want awakened
Take me

The rose knows only sun and warmth
It touched my face
It filled my heart
Take me, take me

Leave that flower
To touch this earth
Take me,
To me that's what
That rose was worth

For me…
It was the only road left
To show my love

Day 5 – June 25th

I tried to reach Z later on Thursday and again on Friday. I hadn't heard from her. I didn't know if she wanted to see me, or if she even wanted to talk to me anymore. I didn't know if she was aware that I'd called the police and the rest of what happened the last couple of days from my end. What I found out the next week was that she had been busy with her apartment for a few days getting the front door taken care of and she was preparing to move.

Day 6 – June 26th

On Saturday, I was working at the supermarket. That was an all-day thing from 10 am to 6 pm. At around noon, I was paged to the courtesy desk at the front of the store. Zorina was there.

I wasn't sure what she was going to say or do. She apologized to me for bothering me at work, then she handed me a 45rpm record. It was Lou Rawls' "You'll Never Find Another Love Like Mine." It was a very recent huge hit all over the airwaves. I thanked her for it and asked her how she was.

We spoke for a couple of minutes, and she seemed okay, although she did say she'd had a terrible headache from Thursday to Friday. She mentioned to me that she'd written me a letter, but I told her I hadn't received it yet. We agreed to talk soon, and I'd let her know when I got that letter. She headed out of the store, and I went back to stocking shelves. It was good to see her and talk to her. When I got home after work the letter was waiting for me with a postmark of the 25th. Here is some of what she wrote to me:

After what happened these past few days, there is no excuse for me. I should be ashamed of myself and I am. That's why I am writing this because no matter how you put it you were at fault too. You put me through hell back and forth. I wish that you realized that I had feelings too because all I ever thought about was your feelings. I should have realized that I should never have put your experience with mine. So, you see we're both at fault. I hope that you'll take this letter into consideration and forgive me, and we could leave everything on only a friendly basis. If it's not too much to ask I wish that on Sundays, you'll let me see your softball games. Please be friends and forget... that this nightmare will go away. I'm promising you on (2) persons that I adore that I will stick to my word. I'm sorry that I'm being a pain in the you know what!

If you ever need anybody to talk to or you need a friend around remember what I always told you. You will always have a friend in me, and I will never let you down. So, when your pretty eyes are full with tears or the sound of this cruel world is driving you crazy baby don't worry. I will always be there and try to make things right for you. So, when you feel like crying and there is no one who has the time to sit and ask you why... when you need someone to hear you or just be near you baby, I will be close by and you can come to talk to me as a friend.

My love will always be with you.   - Z

She had apologized to me again, but she hadn't done anything wrong. It was all my fault. I should be the one apologizing to her. All she did was love me with everything inside of her, and I broke her heart. I called her after I read the letter and thanked her. I told her I'd like it if she would still come to my games, and that I was sorry about things the past month.

I read that letter a couple of times, and I looked at that 45rpm she had handed to me. I hoped she wasn't right about "You'll Never Find Another Love Like Mine." We were still in love with each other, but on a personal basis we'd reached a different level. Decades later, I would tell a few friends about those six days in June and how much we loved each other. I would also say there was a bond between us that could never be broken. That bond was formed in a life and death situation, and it remains to this day.

Things were about to change in our relationship. We were slowing things down a bit. We still loved and needed each other, but we both finally realized that our situation was out of the ordinary. This was 1976 and society still frowned upon an older woman with a younger guy, especially if she was divorced with children.

She was about to start protecting her heart, and I was about to grow up very quickly on an emotional level. To this day, my parents don't know what happened that June. I'd made up my mind that I was going to do what I decided was right for myself. If my life or someone else's life was going to be impacted by something, I did or said, then it would all be on me. I'd only have myself to thank, or I'd be kicking myself in the ass for screwing things up. I promised myself I would never hurt another girl like that again, not ever. Six years later I would keep that promise.

The second paragraph above that she wrote in her letter to me would be something that I would seriously wonder about forty-three years later. There's a long way to go here. I promise that I'll cover it when I get to 2019. And in case you're wondering, yes, I still have Lou Rawls' 45 that she gave me. On the label she wrote, *To Mike*. She underlined the song title.

By early the next week, we got together. She wanted to show me the apartment she and her kids were going to be moving into. The apartment was vacant, and she would be moving in within the next week. The incident with the police and the emergency services people breaking down her door the week before caused a problem for her. The building manager made her leave due to what happened with the paramedics, so she had to move.

At about the same time, I was leaving my job at the supermarket after July 4th since I was working the summer job forty hours a week. The beaches had already been open for a month, and we were looking forward to enjoying some time there together over the summer. Z & I weren't seeing each other as often as we had been, but neither of us could walk away from the other. We were somehow going to try to make our relationship work. The one thing that was an obstacle was the situation we were in. As far as our love for one another went, there was no problem there.

With that said, I wanted to figure out what I wanted in the long term. I told Zorina I wanted to date other girls. I didn't have anyone in particular that I wanted to see, I just wanted to find out for myself how committed I was in our relationship. I know that sounds a bit crazy, actually immature, but she was the first girl that I'd had a real relationship with. When I told her that, she said this to me.

"If it's okay for you to date other girls, would it be okay for me to date other guys?" Then she said, "If you don't want me to date other guys, I won't."

Well, the fair thing to do was for me to say it was okay for her to date other guys, so my inner "Richie" came through, and I said it was okay. We didn't see each other that coming weekend, which just happened to be America's bicentennial. She was busy moving and getting settled in at her new apartment, and I was working my last Saturday at the supermarket. We weren't intimately involved any longer at this point. We were still getting together a couple of days a week, hitting Jones Beach every couple of weeks with friends, and maybe going out for an evening to a club to dance and have a few drinks.

I dated a couple of girls over the next month. It just didn't feel right. There wasn't a connection with them for me, and I missed Z so much when I wasn't with her. I was beginning to understand what she had been trying to explain to me the last few months.

On August 22nd we went with some friends to Jones Beach. I have a dated photo that I took that day of her sitting on one of my friend's shoulders. It's a frozen moment in time.

It was a couple of weeks later that my friend Jerry asked me to come over to listen to Chicago's new album Chicago X . I just now checked its release date, and as a matter of "coincidence", it had been released on my birthday two months before.

The first few songs played, and then the song "If You Leave Me Now" came on. Although I hadn't heard it on the radio yet, it was released as a single on July 31st. When it was done playing, I asked Jerry to play it again. I ended up asking him to play it at least four times in a row. Each time I listened to it, I was learning from it.

It was explaining to me what Zorina had been trying to tell me. The last time that I asked him to play it, the proverbial light bulb came on for me. It was as if a thousand-piece crossword puzzle fell out of the sky and all the pieces just fell into place. I sat there for a couple of minutes and asked myself, what the hell have I been doing? That's what she's been trying to tell me. I'm in love with Zorina. I don't care that she's older than me, or that she has kids, or that she's divorced, and I don't care who doesn't like any of that. I love her, and I have to tell her all of those things.

As soon as I got hold of her, I told her I wanted to see her, that I had something very important to tell her. It was very early September, and I was going to make a commitment to her.

The next day, I went over to her place. I was so excited, and I told her how Chicago's song, "If You Leave Me Now", made me understand everything. I told her how much I loved her, and that I didn't care about anything except our being together. I told her that she had been right about us, and that I wanted to make a commitment to her and start making plans for a future together. I said marriage should wait until I got a job that could support us, but once I finished college next June, things should begin to happen for us.

She listened to everything I had to say. Then she told me she was getting a job and bringing in a roommate to help with the bills. Then she said she'd given our relationship a lot of thought and due to our different places in life, that we shouldn't continue dating.

In a very helpless manner, I said, "But I understand now what you were trying to tell me."

Zorina had reached the same point that I had reached a couple of months earlier, questioning whether this relationship would ever work. It may possibly have been a bit of pride on her part as well to turn me away, but I think the bulk of it was actually a realization on her part that we wouldn't be accepted as a couple. She knew I was serious about what I'd said to her, and I believed that she was still in love with me.

She said the job would take up most of her time, and there were bills from her hospitalization that she needed to take care of. She seemed like she was hedging just a bit on us not seeing each other again, then she said maybe in the spring we might try again if we're both still interested. I was now at her mercy the way she had been at mine a couple of months before. I had no option but to agree to her wishes.

It was early September, and as I stated before, God hadn't accepted my original end of the deal by taking me in place of Zorina. My payment for her full recovery was about to start.

Chapter Four

Over the next five months singer Burton Cummings and comedian Freddie Prinze would indirectly save my life.

The Fall/Winter of 1976

As September took hold, so did a deep depression inside of me. I missed Z very much. I tried to call her a few times, but either there was no answer or her roommate would answer and tell me Z didn't want to speak to me. I was like a drug addict who couldn't get a sorely needed fix. Big Sal and I were hanging out together more often during this time. I needed someone to lean on, and as it turned out, a girl that he had been dating broke up with him recently as well, so we helped each other. Sal was a big, tough, no-nonsense guy when it came to his bouncer job at the clubs, but I'd known him since we were eleven years old, and he was just a big softy with a big heart when it came down to it.

It does amaze me that certain songs were big hits on the radio during this entire timeframe that somehow seemed to fit right in with what was going on in my relationship with Zorina. In September, the song, "She's Gone", by Hall & Oates was huge, and I related to it very closely from having screwed up my relationship with Z.

Things got much worse for me by October. I'd quit the supermarket job in early July, and the summer job ended at the end of September. I hadn't taken any fall classes and wasn't sure that I would continue college to earn my degree. I was becoming self-destructive. I was very edgy and depressed. The thought of Z consumed me in my waking hours, and I was literally crying myself to sleep nearly every night.

My first thoughts of ending my life began in October. I couldn't function. I had no interest in anything or anybody except for her. This would be the first of four times in my life that, in effect, she would consume my being, my soul.

Sometime around late October or early November, Burton Cummings put out a new song called, "Stand Tall". It became an anthem for me. It was helping me deal with not having Zorina in my life. It lowered the level of depression and anxiety that I had been feeling. Just stand tall for one more day and then another day after that.

A friend of mine named Joey had been dating a girl since the summer. I saw him one evening, and he told me they stopped seeing each other a month earlier. I asked him if he'd mind if I asked her out. He was okay with that, so I contacted her.

Marissa was a junior in high school. She was a beautiful strawberry blonde, and she was a ballerina. Needless to say, she was very thin, but she had class and style and she looked great in cutoff jeans.

We dated about a half dozen times through early January. I just wasn't ready to date yet, so we stopped seeing each other. I couldn't keep my mind off of Z, although I did get a Christmas card from her, which really picked me up. I was signing up for spring classes and was looking into getting a job in town at a leather factory. I was setting all my classes up for evenings so I could work days.

It was January, the dead of winter. "Stand Tall" was still helping me face each day, but I was slowly losing the battle. Again, I had thoughts of ending my life. I was and still am a bit of a neat freak, so anything that would be messy just wasn't for me—no car wrecks, no guns, no jumping off of buildings or bridges. I was afraid of heights anyway. Remember?

I'm not trying to make light of being depressed and on edge, but these were actually things I took into consideration. I was struggling very badly emotionally. So many nights, I'd ask God to please don't let me wake up in the morning…and then I'd wake up and have to face another day. Valentine's Day was only a couple of weeks away, and I wanted to take Zorina out for an evening, but she still wouldn't even speak to me.

Then, something happened that got my attention. Something that made me understand that I had a future, and I needed to be strong to make that future a reality.

Freddie Prinze was a very talented and likeable comedian who had a hit TV show. He was twenty-two years old, just a year older than me. One day, in late January 1977, he shot himself. According to the news media, there had been a problem in his marriage, and he pulled a trigger. A day or two later, he died from his wounds.

Here was this extremely likeable and successful guy that was my age, and now he was gone because his relationship had a problem. I looked at that and thought he had so much to live for. Then I looked at myself and realized I was planning on doing the same type of thing he had done. That gave me something good to think about. I would have a tomorrow, and for the first time in many months, I would be glad to wake up in the morning. I finally understood that taking one's own life was a permanent solution to a temporary problem.

Valentine's Day came and went, and I was starting that factory job and began night classes. Having those things to do helped occupy my mind, but Z was still consuming me. I had no one to blame but myself, and that's what ate away at me more than anything.

I kept thinking that if I had come to my senses a month earlier, by the end of July she would have said yes to me, and we'd still be together. Spring was about a month away. I hoped that maybe she would be contacting me by April to start seeing each other again, but that only seemed like a pipe dream. I had to accept that she was gone and going on with her life, and I needed to do the same.

Then, in late March, I got a phone call from Zorina. She had been working as a barmaid all these months, and she told me where she worked. It was a social club, and she told me to come by and see her.

Over the next month, I stopped in there a few times, but we really couldn't talk much since she was working. She was really good at tending bar, meaning she had a personality that people just gravitated to. She was very personable. We talked on the phone quite a bit during this time, and things seemed good between us.

By late April or early May, she invited me to come over to her apartment. When I got there, she was ready to have a conversation about us dating again to see how things would go with us. I didn't hide the fact that I was still in love with her, and it seemed that she still felt that way about me after all these months.

In familiar fashion, she put a 45 on the record player while we were talking. It was Andy Gibbs' "I Just Want To Be Your Everything." I got the message loud and clear, and I told her I'd do everything and anything to get our relationship back on track. She wrote a dedication to me on the record label.

To Mike with all my Love, from Zorina.

Of course, I still have that 45!

Finally, I had that second chance to get this right. I knew I needed to be more involved with her kids, so when she was working in the evening, and she couldn't get someone to stay with them, I'd go over there and watch Jeannette and Luca until she got home, usually no later than about 11:00. It was May, and we were going out a couple of evenings a week just spending time together. We weren't physically involved, and that really didn't matter to me. I wanted her heart again. I wanted her to open up to me and give of herself when she was ready.

One evening in May, we went over to Boy Boy's disco. Big Sal was there and so were a few other people we knew. The place wasn't very crowded, so it must have been a weekday, maybe a Wednesday or Thursday. The DJ was spinning records, and he put on Englebert's latest hit "After The Lovin' ".

Z and I jumped up and headed for the dance floor. We were the only two out there. I held her close, and she looked up at me with those big dark eyes. I leaned over slightly, and she got up on her toes, and we kissed for a few seconds. Then she laid her head on my chest, and we just lived in the moment.

I have to say that I've experienced winning races and softball championships when I was still competing, getting married, having children, watching a beautiful sunset in the Caribbean, had my favorite sports teams win world championships numerous times. I even saw Mickey Mantle in person on Memorial Day weekend 1968 go 5 for 5 with two homers, but those few minutes… those few minutes on the dance floor with Zorina was and still is a moment in time that surpasses all of them. It was like Heaven on earth. She didn't say it, but she didn't have to. She was still in love with me.

We couldn't wait to get to the beaches, so on Memorial Day weekend the two of us headed out to Jones beach for a day. The water was cold, but it was a really nice day and a bit windy. I have a photo that a stranger took of us with our backs to the water. It's dated 5-28-77.

Things were very good with us. My birthday was in a couple of weeks, so I wanted to do something special to celebrate it with her. Okay now, remember this is June 1977. Englebert was still big, as was Elvis, Sinatra, and a guy named Tom Jones. Z loved all of those guys. So, we were going to go out for dinner first, then I got us two tickets for a Tom Jones show in Tarrytown at an indoor venue on June 16th. The venue only seated about 3,000 people, so no matter where you sat, you had a great seat.

Okay, okay. I admit it. We were about five rows from the back of the place, but it was sold out, and our tickets only cost…and this is for real…$8.50 each. How do I remember? Come on! I still have my original ticket stub!

Jones put on a great show. The women in the audience were throwing their bras and panties at him. A few of them even gave him bouquets of roses. Z and I had a great time, and things seemed to be getting back to normal for us.

Sometime in late June or early July, I took Z's son, Luca, to a Yankee game. I asked if Jeannette wanted to go too, but Z said she wouldn't be interested in it, so it was just me and Luca on a guy's day out.

I can't remember who the Yanks played that day, or if they even won or lost, but we had seats in the upper deck about twenty rows back. I don't know how they sell tickets to these events, but the first ten rows of the upper deck were empty on the left field side where we were sitting, so we walked right down to the front row and sat there a while right on the rail. We did the soda, hot dogs, and peanuts thing, and were enjoying the game.

The one thing that stands out in my mind about that day was a foul ball that came up to where we were sitting in the upper front row. We both stood up to try to catch it. It just about made the railing. We both reached for it, but it hit the rail and fell down to the lower deck. We just looked at each other like why didn't you catch that? We had a good laugh about it.

We got to do something together, just the two of us, and it was a good day. I wanted to be and needed to be more a part of Z's kid's lives. I wanted to let Zorina know that I understood this wasn't just about the two of us. I was ready to take on her kids as well, and I hoped at some point we'd be a family.

At this point, I hadn't told my parents that Zorina and I were dating again. I wanted for us to make a commitment to each other and know where we were headed before I told Mom & Dad. That way I could say *this is a done deal and we're planning a future together*. I was still working full time at the factory and making decent money. I graduated in June with a degree in Business/Real Estate. Yes, a degree in Real Estate. That was a new curriculum at my college.

In July, things were still going well with us, but Z wasn't opening up to me emotionally. I wondered if she might be afraid to give her heart to me again. There was a closeness and a love between us that I could feel and at times I could see her wanting to open herself up to me, but she just kept holding back. I let her know that I was all in, that I wanted us to have a life together along with her kids, we'd be a family. I have a couple of photos of us from a day at the beach in July at Glen Island, and we were still going places together a couple of days a week.

Sometime in early July, I got a call from Connie. She and her friend Donna were going to take a trip to NY City for a week to see the sights. Connie had signed up for a five-year stint in the Peace Corps somewhere in East Asia, so she decided she wanted to see the big city before she left the country.

I told Connie how Z and I were back together and trying to make things work. I told Zorina what was going on, and that Connie and her friend were just coming up from the city for one day to see me in early August. As it turned out, they were planning to visit me on a Sunday when Boy Boy's was playing a softball game against another bar. Z knew one of the guys on the other team, so she got a ride with him. I arrived with Connie and Donna who had taken a train north, and I picked them up at the train station. Connie and Zorina got to meet each other, and it was a fun game. We won something like 26 – 24. Scoring runs in slow pitch softball can get a bit out of control. I so liked showing off for Zorina, and that day was no different. I hit two homers and one was a grand slam.

One afternoon, about a week later, I heard a news report on the radio. The rock'n roll world suffered a big loss. Elvis Presley had died. As soon as I heard it, I called Z and told her. She hadn't heard the news yet. As I was telling her, she turned on the TV to see if she could get any more details.

She said, "No, no. You're not serious."

I had to tell her it was true. She loved Elvis as so many people did.

I was twenty-two years old. I was in love. I had a decent job. I knew what I wanted in life, and I was so glad to be alive.

Chapter Five

I loved Z, and I know she loved me, but she just couldn't seem to let her heart open up to me again. After what she'd been through the year before, it was understandable. Whenever we went anywhere, we always sat right next to one another so we were touching at the hips or the shoulders, or she'd have her arm wrapped around mine. It was like we were energizing each other by being in physical contact, and yet we couldn't seem to take that final step to close the deal. Maybe she needed more time.

I don't remember exactly when things began to fizzle with us, but it was around mid-August. At that time, I wasn't sure why things fell apart. There was a barrier there that I couldn't break through, so I went about my life, and she went about hers. After that, we would see each other every month or so when I would stop in to have a drink where she was working. Sometimes I would be there when she finished her shift. She would come sit next to me, and we'd talk for a while. Sometimes I'd even take her home.

It was late August '77, soon after things with me & Z seemed to come to a standstill. I had done some shopping, and I was getting in my car in a parking lot when a car pulled up.

A female shouted, "Hi, how have you been?"

It was Marissa. We talked for a few minutes. I asked her if she'd like to do something together soon, and she said yes. The beaches were open for a couple of more weekends, so that's where we headed the coming weekend.

We started hanging out together more often and dating through September. Things were going very well. I missed Z, but Marissa was able to keep my mind occupied. Her family was well off, and she'd traveled quite a bit even outside the U.S. She had style, class, elegance, and a maturity beyond her years, but she was just starting her senior year in high school.

I went for a job interview in early October with a major corporation. They hired me on as a temporary 90-day hire.

Her Dad liked the way my car was always clean and waxed, so he'd pay me $50 every couple of weeks to detail his car. Of course, the money would get spent on his daughter, so it was a win/win for him. Even though her parents liked me, I felt like I was the kid from the wrong side of the tracks.

My friends and my parent's friends were blue-collar working class types, good people, the working with your hands, beer-drinking types, so it was a completely different lifestyle than what Marissa was used to. Her parents would have dinner parties. They were very nice gatherings with doctors, lawyers, Indian Chiefs (Just kidding. There were no Indian Chiefs), and professors, etc, You know, the tweed jacket, bearded, pipe-smoking types. They were all very nice people, but just different than what I was used to.

You've heard the saying, "So this is how the other half lives." Well, I was seeing how the other half lived. I kind of liked it…a lot. Fortunately, I'd just started with that company, so I had some kind of standing along with the business/real estate degree I'd earned a few months before to play myself up a bit. I'd try to move on right away to another person at their parties before they could ask what type of position I had with the company. Admitting that I was working in the mail room was something I tried desperately to avoid.

Sometime in early November, Marissa's Dad got four tickets to see *Dracula* on Broadway. So, here I was headed out for my first dinner in Manhattan and a Broadway show. Things went very well. The ambience of the theatre was like stepping back in time. The architecture and the style was something you'd normally only see in the movies. The play was rolling along, and then things just stopped. They drew the curtains closed. It was halftime…I mean intermission!

Most people went for drinks or to the rest rooms for that twenty minutes. The restrooms were upstairs. There was this very wide, curved staircase, like something you'd see in *Gone With The Wind*. As I was heading back down the stairs, coming up with his daughter, was actor Cliff Robertson.

Robertson played JFK in the movie *PT 109*. I couldn't believe it was him. I was looking straight at him, and he made eye contact with me as we were passing each other, shoulder to shoulder. I just smiled with an I-know-who-you-are look on my face, and he smiled back. I couldn't wait to tell Marissa and her parents. The rest of the evening went well, and was very memorable.

I missed Zorina, and as I said, I would see her once in a while when she was working. It seemed that both of us needed that little bit of time together to get our fixes of each other. Our relationship had become a "just friends" type of thing, but I always felt that there was an underlying, unspoken thing between us. She was always in my heart. She seemed to be doing well, and we were living our lives…apart from each other.

Marissa and I were steadies now, and I became more focused on her. She was beginning to touch my heart as well. At Thanksgiving, her parents invited me over to have dinner with them. Again, this was not just a regular family turkey day.

They had a woman that would come in on special occasions to prepare things and cook dinner. It was all very elegant with the finest china and crystal glasses. It was my first experience with twice baked potatoes. Were they ever good!

Marissa was preparing for a performance of *The Nutcracker Suite* that her ballet company was going to put on for Christmas. She was the prima ballerina, so she would be the Sugar Plum Fairy, and she was practicing very hard after Thanksgiving. Her performance would be about a week before Christmas.

I attended the performance with her parents, and it was perfect. I really was very proud of her, understanding the dedication and effort that went into it. We spent Christmas Eve together, and Christmas day I spent with my family as she did with hers. We'd been dating for about four months, and she'd met my parents once or twice.

I wasn't one to bring a girl home to meet the family right away. Zorina had been the first one I'd ever brought home, and that had been about a month into that relationship.

Marissa and I were frequent patrons at Boy Boy's disco. She liked the friendly atmosphere and the fact that I was friends with a bunch of the guys who hung out there, since quite a few of us played softball together on the team. Big Sal was always an entertaining force and was very personable. Most of the other guys had girlfriends, as well, that would be there.

On New Year's Eve, there was a party at Boy Boy's, so we attended that. It was a really nice and fun evening and was the first New Year's Eve that I'd ever gone out to a club. We rang in 1978 together and rented a motel room for the night. In the morning, we went out for breakfast, then I took her home.

In early January, my 90-day temporary employment with that corporation was coming to an end. I'd worked hard, working overtime on weekdays and weekends. I was banking my regular paycheck and living on my overtime check. I was very dedicated, and I really wanted to be hired full-time. With two days to go before my employment was up, the manager called me in. I knew he was going to tell me that either I was being released, or I was being hired as a full-time employee.

It was the latter, and I was so excited. This was a career move, and I'd end up being with them over twenty-five years.

I was really starting to get emotionally involved with Marissa. We were very comfortable with each other. I wanted to get her something special for Valentine's Day, so I went to a nearby jewelry store.

I was looking at rings. You know, something she could wear when we went out, not an everyday ring to wear. I found one that had two hearts intertwined with a small diamond chip in the middle. When she wore it, she liked to hold her left hand out and display it so everybody and anybody could see it. We were seeing each other a few days a week, and things were cruising along for us.

Spring break came along in March that year, and Marissa and a bunch of her female high school classmates went down to Florida for the week. I had talked to Zorina and taken the opportunity for us to get together one evening during that week. She knew I'd been dating someone for quite a few months.

We went over to Boy Boy's on a Friday night and hung out with Big Sal and a couple of other people. We had some drinks and some laughs. Sal told his jokes and stories, and it was just really nice to spend time with her. It was the first time since August that we'd gone somewhere together.

At one point, the DJ played the song "If I Can't Have You". As the song played, Z looked at me and sang a couple of lines. I really didn't think much about it until after we left Boy Boy's. Things wound down for the evening, and we headed for my car.

I let Z in the passenger side, and she unlocked the driver side for me. I was warming up the car for a few minutes, and we were talking. She leaned in toward me and kissed me…and I kissed her back. I wasn't expecting that from her, but I did my part in return. She just smiled at me when we were done.

I wasn't sure what to make of it, but it seemed like a spontaneous moment. We didn't have any conversation about dating again or anything like that. I took her home, then I went home. I began to feel guilty about that kiss, since I was dating Marissa now. I decided not to say anything about it to Marissa, since nothing else went on between me and Z.

Marissa's vacation ended, and she had a nice tan from her trip. A few days later, one of her girlfriends pulled me aside and told me Marissa had cheated on me while she was in Florida. She'd slept with another guy. I was pretty upset, and now that stolen kiss with Z didn't seem like such a big deal anymore.

The next day I confronted Marissa about it, and to her credit she owned up to it, but at the same time she acted as if it was no big deal. That didn't set well with me. Within a couple of weeks, we broke up. It was mid-April.

We ended up getting together a couple of times through early July, but we were no longer on the same page about things, so it really ended at that point. I don't remember how or why Z and I didn't give it another shot. We'd been living our lives and both of us seemed to be okay with the way things were. I dated a few other girls over the rest of the summer, but nothing was serious.

My cousin James and I would go out to the different clubs, and on the weekends, we'd try to hit Jones Beach. I wasn't really interested in dating anyone on a steady basis in late '78. The last two years had been an emotionally draining period of time for me. My relationship with Zorina was over, and Marissa hurt me with her lack of seriousness. She was just too young, too wild, and too wealthy to feel that she should get herself tied down to just one guy at the age of eighteen.

At work, a new girl entered my life. Anna Lee was very pretty, just over five feet tall, about a hundred pounds, dark-haired, dark-eyed, and was Spanish. You get the picture…in a lot of ways very similar to Z.

I wasn't really interested, not because I didn't think that she was a little hottie, but because I was in need of a break from the emotional roller coaster I'd been on. We talked a bit, and I really began to like her. She was hard working, very sensible, and seemed to pay a lot of attention to me. After a couple of months, we began dating. I would still drop in to see Z at her job, once in a while, and I still hoped she would begin to open up to me, but things hadn't changed with us.

Anna Lee and I began dating on a regular basis. She cared for me very much and was very loyal and focused on a relationship with me. It finally became an exclusive relationship. I trusted her, and she was very giving of herself, something that Marissa hadn't been with me. It was the same cultural thing that Zorina had exhibited, and I liked it very much.

Through 1979 into 1980, we dated, and I thought maybe she would be the right one for me, the one that I'd been waiting for. I told her about my relationship with Zorina and what had happened there. She was very understanding about it. She even asked if sometime she might be able to meet Z. I said sure, okay.

Around mid '80, I was thinking that I might ask Anna Lee, at some point in the near future, to marry me. It was sometime in the summer of '80 that Anna Lee and I met Zorina at Eddie's Bar. I was a bit uncomfortable about it at first, but both of them seemed to be getting along just "peachy" at the bar. They both spoke fluent Spanish, so they were yacking away for over an hour.

I couldn't understand what they were saying and felt left out. When Anna Lee and I left the bar, I asked her what she and Z had talked about. She said they talked about a lot of different things, and that Z had told her how lucky she was to have a guy like me, and that I was such a good guy. They had talked for a long time, so I felt pretty sure there was quite a bit more to it, but Anna Lee wasn't offering any more info about their conversation.

A few months later we were having some problems, and we stopped seeing each other. I was a free man again, and I had the dating field open to me.

Re-enter Marissa in the late summer of '80.

We had run into one another at a local bar one evening and got to talking. Marissa was twenty years old now, and I thought maybe she might be ready to have a serious relationship. Over about a three-week period, we went out a few times.

This was the third time in four years that we'd dated. It wasn't serious or involved this time. We were just getting a feel for one another again. One night in late September, I saw her at a local place we both frequented. She was alone at the bar, and of course we got to talking. She went on to relate to me how she met some guy at a bar the week before and they hooked up. At that moment, I realized that she hadn't changed a bit. We talked a little while longer, and I headed out of the bar. I'd made up my mind that I was never going to get together with her again.

Fall had come, and Anna Lee and I still weren't dating. I missed her, but I was trying to figure out what I wanted for my life. Marissa was a done deal, Anna Lee was at least on-hold, and Zorina was not an option.

Z and I would still see each other and talk when I stopped in to where she worked. I told her that Anna Lee and I weren't dating anymore. Z and I hadn't gone anywhere together since March of '78. In December of '80, Zorina asked me to come by her apartment. Things quickly went to a place that I wasn't expecting. We had an intimate evening, but it just didn't feel right for me. That wasn't what I wanted from her. I wanted her heart again, but it had only been a physical thing that evening. It bothered me that that's all it was. There was no talk about dating again.

Chapter Six

In late January, Anna Lee and I began dating again. The break we had taken seemed to have been good for both of us, and we were both glad to be together again. Things were going well, and a couple of months later, I asked her to marry me.

She wanted a June wedding, but with June three months away, there wasn't enough time or availability of venues to do it that quick, so we decided that June the following year would be okay. About a week later, I got a call from Marissa. She heard from friends that I had gotten engaged.

She said "Hi", then the next thing she said was, "Where have you been for the last six months?"

I responded, "Did you just notice I was gone?"

Needless to say, the conversation went downhill from there. I told her what I really thought of her, and the conversation ended fairly quickly. I would never see her or even talk to her ever again…and I didn't care one damn bit.

It was 1981, and life was just cruising along. Anna Lee and I were doing very well and beginning to plan things for next year. I'd still drop in to see Z once in a while at her job. As soon as I had gotten engaged, I told Zorina about it. I thought she might be a bit taken aback by it, but she seemed very happy for me. It had been five years since we'd originally dated and four years since we'd gotten back together for a few months in '77.

I began thinking that maybe I had been holding on emotionally with her even though she hadn't shown an emotional interest in me in four years. Deep down inside though, I still felt that she was still in love with me. Whenever I would go see her, there still seemed to be an unspoken thing between us on an emotional level. I couldn't shake that feeling, but as time went by, I slowly began to feel more and more that maybe it was just my male ego at work. And yet, I would still feel re-energized when I was in her presence as if some type of invisible force was re-charging me.

Well, 1982 finally rolled in. The wedding was six months away, and we were getting ready for that. Every month or so, I would still drop in for a beer, see Z, then I'd be on my way again. We were friends. That's all it had been for so long with us. I'd still do anything for her if she asked, and she'd do anything for me as well.

I never knew if she was dating or anything like that. It's not something we would ever discuss. She had her life, and I had mine. We'd see each other once in a while at her place of business. That was it.

The months kept passing by, and June finally came around. We had invited Z to attend the wedding, but she declined the invitation. About a week before the wedding, I stopped in to see Zorina one last time before I got married. She was working, and we just talked about everyday things. When she finished her shift about an hour after I got there, she came around the bar, and sat next to me.

We talked for another half hour or so. You know how there are certain moments in your life that you just remember where you were, who you were with, and what was said? For me, this was and still is one of those moments. It's right up there with the day JFK was shot and the day the Twin Towers came down.

Zorina was sitting on my right, she turned toward me, reached over, and put her right hand on my right forearm. I looked into her big, dark eyes, and she was focused on mine as well.

Then, she said, "Michael, if you change your mind about getting married this weekend, we'll go back out again." She hesitated for just a second, and added, "And then, we'll get married."

I just sat there speechless for probably about ten seconds. I was still focused on her eyes, then I slightly turned my head away. I was trying to process what she had just said to me.

I turned my head back toward her and said, "I've been waiting nearly six years for you to say that or even anything like that." Still dazed, I said, "The wedding is this weekend."

I don't remember saying "no" to her, but I certainly didn't tell her, okay we're back together now.

Then she said, "Well, if you change your mind, we'll go out again."

I don't remember any of the conversation we had after that. I finally headed home and was as confused and unsure of myself as I'd been in years.

I think between her being initially somewhat emotionally afraid to get back together with me in '77, convincing herself for years that it would never work, and maybe even denying to herself that she was still in love with me was why we'd stayed apart. So, I had been right all those years about her. She *was* still in love with me, and even though I loved Anna Lee and was getting married, I was still in love with Zorina.

Two days later, I was with Anna Lee. I told her that I wasn't sure that I wanted to go through with the wedding. She didn't say anything. She looked away and looked out the window. She was like that for about thirty seconds, then she turned back toward me. She was very hurt, and her eyes had welled up. She wasn't sure what to say or what to do.

Finally, she asked me if I was testing her. At that moment, I remembered what I had promised myself six years earlier, that I would never hurt anybody again the way I had hurt Zorina.

I answered Anna Lee's question, "No, I'm not testing you. It's just a big step in life, and I'm nervous about it. It's okay. We'll be okay. It's alright."

The wedding went on as planned, and we went on our honeymoon. About a month after the wedding, I stopped in to see Z at the bar. She had just gotten off her shift, and we made our way over to one of the tables. She went over to the juke box and played the Gap band's song "You Dropped A Bomb On Me".

She came back over to the table, looked at me, and in a very deliberate tone she said exactly that, "You dropped a bomb on me."

I said, "Now, hold on. I was engaged for over a year, and you knew I was engaged the whole time, so don't try to put this all on me. And besides, you met Anna Lee a couple of years ago and told her how lucky she was to be with me."

She thought about what I said for a couple of seconds, and she sat down. She knew I was right. That didn't make her feel any better about things. We talked for a while, though I don't really remember any more of that conversation either. There was one thing I wanted to tell her, but I knew it was better that I didn't. I never told her that I nearly backed out of the wedding to Anna Lee. It was just pointless to tell her. We'd known each other for over six years. We still loved each other. Neither one of us had been able to get our relationship back together, and now…I was married.

Within a couple of months, Anna Lee and I got settled in. Summer was ending, and we were making a life a together. I didn't see Zorina as often now, not that I saw her very often before my marriage. Physically, it was just a friendship thing between us, but emotionally there was still that underlying knowledge that we had strong feelings for each other.

In midwinter, Anna Lee was going out of town for a few days. I contacted Z and asked if she'd like to get together for an evening for drinks and a bite to eat.

Let me make something perfectly clear right now. At no time during my marriage to Anna Lee did anything, not anything, not so much as a stolen kiss occurred between me and Zorina. Our feelings ran very deep for each other, but we didn't cross that line in the sand.

On Saturday night, I picked Zorina up, and we went to a local place. They had good food and a dance floor so we were there for a couple of hours. We talked about what was going on in each other's lives, and we reminisced a bit about our previous relationship.

We danced a few dances, a couple of faster ones, and a slow one. It did feel good to hold her. There was still that energy between us when we were together…like no one and nothing could come between us. We finally left and headed for my car.

It was winter, so I was warming it up for a few minutes. I couldn't keep my silence any longer. I told her how much I missed her, and that I was still in love with her. I wasn't trying for a cheap thrill, and I wasn't lying to her. What I said came from the heart, and she knew it. I told her I wanted to marry her, and I'd get a divorce. She just sat there, and covered her face with her hands, and began crying.

"Why are you doing this to me?" she asked.

All I could do was answer her question with complete honesty. "Because I'm still in love with you."

She asked me to take her home, so I did.

It was around this time that I needed an emotional outlet, so I began to write my thoughts down in the form of poetry. Words just flowed out of me. Some of it wasn't very good, most of it was mediocre at best, but I think some of it was better than average. I didn't show Z any of the things that I was writing about her. They weren't meant to win her over or anything like that, they were personal to me to try to keep myself sane, to get my feelings out of my head, and put them someplace else. I wrote the following poem within a week after Z and I had gone out that evening.

Times

It seems so long ago at times
And at times like yesterday
Since we spent our time together
Sharing love from day to day

When I think how good it was to hold you
That seems so long ago
But when I think about the love we had
I just want you to know

That time does not destroy true love
The good times and the bad
It somehow seems to make you dream
You reflect from glad to sad

Then you begin to wonder about
The things that used to be
The time we had to spend together
The times of you and me

Time can't take those things away
It just keeps them in our minds
Too often I miss those days with you
Thinking about you from time to time

It was a few months later before I saw Z again. As usual, she was working on a Sunday afternoon, and I stopped in. This time it was for more than just a beer. I had more than just chit chat to talk about.

Remember that pinky ring I mentioned earlier that she wanted to wear when we were dating back in '76, but I'd given her another ring to wear instead?

On this day, I had it on my pinkie, and before I left, I said, "I have something for you that you always wanted."

She watched me take it off, and I said, "Here. This is yours. You always loved it and wanted it, and I'm giving it to you."

She accepted it, but at the same time, I could see she realized the seriousness of what I was really saying to her. She understood that it represented "all my love". Then I told her I had something else for her, that if anything ever happened to me, my cousin James had instructions to see that she got it. At that moment, Zorina's slightly warped sense of humor made an appearance.

She asked, "Is it going to be a part of your body?"

It was a lighthearted moment, and I sheepishly said, "No. It's not a part of my body, but you'll love it anyway."

All I said was that it was a box of personal things, and I left it at that. At the beginning of this story, I mentioned that although I don't have a diary, I did keep many things. As of that day, there were cards and letters she had given me, mementos from places we'd gone together, music records she'd given me. a couple that I'd gotten for her, and the poem I had just recently written about her.

As the years went by, I would add more things to that box. You have to understand…I felt that I would be the first one to leave this earth since she'd already died, and by the Grace of God she was revived before crossing over to the other side. When I finally left this earth, that box of items was to be hers to let her know, without any doubts, that I had truly loved her as much as she'd loved me. That was its purpose.

Now, I'd given her that ring, and she knew I was getting very emotionally attached again. Then, there was the promise of a box of personal things if something were to happen to me. I got off my seat at the bar, and said, "I'll see you around."

She said *see you*, and I left to go home.

I stopped in a few more times to see Z over the next few months. She knew that I wanted us to be together again, and she had been wearing the ring I had given her. In August, I stopped in and she had some news for me.

I noticed she didn't have the ring on her finger. She said she'd met a guy, was getting married, and moving to Florida. I asked her to please reconsider, but she said it was a done deal. I felt as if she was doing it just to get away from me. I mean, what are the odds you're going to meet someone and move out of state?

I know I sound conceited and self-centered, but her family was all right there in the NYC area. Her kids were about nineteen and sixteen years old, and they weren't going to Florida with her. It just didn't seem right to me.

Before I left that day, she played a song on the juke box and dedicated it to me. The song was The Supremes' "Someday We'll Be Together." I was kind of surprised by her choosing that song at that moment, since I was the one who initially screwed things up between us in June of '76. As I listened to it, however, I understood that she knew that when I went to her in early September of '76 and told that I understood everything and wanted to make a life with her, she turned me away. I would reference that song in a poem a few years down the road.

Chapter Seven

By September, Z got married and moved away. I wouldn't see or hear from her again until January '87. During the time she was gone, I went into my second bout of being consumed by her. I went into a deep depression and began writing things down to get them out of my head.

My marriage was surviving so far, but I was beginning to break down emotionally to the point where I once again didn't care if I saw another day. I wrote five poems over about a twelve-month period, when I finally hit bottom with the last one. Here are three full poems and excerpts from two others in the order they were written.

I Remember Yesterday

I remember yesterday
When we used to be
I remember yesterday
When love was you and me

We'd pass our time away
Gaze into each other's eyes
No one knew way back then
How those eyes would cry

Can't help thinking bout you girl
The way I made you cry
The way you hurt me too
When all I did was try

To do the things that were right
That's why I set you free
Though they turned out to be
The wrong things for you and me

Every day that passes now
Feels like eternity
What happened to the world
The world of you and me

Come on back to me now
I need you by my side
Let's erase the memories of
The times that we both cried

Make tomorrow shine
Like all our yesterdays
Let me love you once more girl
In so many ways

I remember yesterday
When we used to be
I remember yesterday
When love was you and me

Excerpt –
There's people all around me
And yet I'm all alone
Just want to hear your soft voice
At the end of a telephone

Someday the hurt will go away
The way I'd like it to
That's the day I'll be at rest
Forever loving you.

Excerpt –
See you on
The other side of midnight
That's where I know
We'll make it alright

See you on
The other side of midnight
That's where I'll be waiting
At the end of the light

She Was

She was "Windy"
She was "Brandy"
She was "Stormy"
She was "Mandy"

She was a rose
She was free
Most of all
She was in love with me

She was so many things
She was so many faces
The real story's told
By the Classic IV's "Traces"

Autumn

As I watch the leaves
Fall in the rain
The autumn is here
I still feel the pain

As the leaves blow away
The wind calls your name
The autumn is here
My tears fall like rain

With you as the teacher
Me learning from you
There's an easier way
As you tried to do

The trees are bare
This autumn's the same
Again life has passed
I feel no more pain

Now the leaves are gone
You're calling my name
Winter has come
Your tears fall like rain

I was barely hanging on. I didn't know how to contact Zorina, and I was very distraught. I kept that to myself, which only heightened the intensity. There wasn't anybody that I could or even wanted to talk to about it. Anna Lee was pregnant with our first child and due in a couple of months.

I know, you must be thinking why didn't he just go on with his life? She married someone else, and she didn't even leave a contact number or address.

I get it, but she was in me, in my heart, in my soul, and I couldn't get her out of my head. I was still in love with her, and as crazy as it sounds, I believed she was still in love with me. Pure insanity, right?

Anna Lee and I had a son, Mickey. It was now early '85, and I had to re-think my life. I had a child, and I wanted to be there for him. That was one of the few things that kept me going. I loved Anna Lee, she loved me, and we were doing okay. The only problem was me, and the only person who could fix that problem was me.

I didn't write anymore about Z in '85 or '86. We had another child in the second half of '86, our daughter, Helen. We were busy working our jobs and changing diapers. You'd be amazed how quickly you can change a diaper after doing it over a thousand times. I was doing well, and so was our marriage when 1987 rolled around.

Chapter Eight

I don't remember how I found out, but by late January '87, I knew that Zorina was back in NY. She'd already been there for about six months. I tried the phone at the apartment she had before she went to Florida since that was the only contact info I had, and she was there. I didn't know it, but her kids had stayed living there while she was away.

I talked to her, and she agreed to get together for a drink soon. By mid-February, I met her at Eddie's. She looked the same, beautiful as ever, and she was wearing a bright red dress. Her long black hair fell down over her shoulders, and she didn't have much makeup on…but then she never needed much anyway. She was a bit overdressed for Eddie's, but I wasn't going to complain! I couldn't take my eyes off her. She just had a way of being tantalizing and exuding a bit of innocence all at the same time. We talked for a while, getting caught up on each other's lives. She told me her marriage fell apart fairly quickly, which didn't surprise me since either my conceit or my confidence told me she was still in love with me.

I know…you're probably still thinking this guy is so full of himself for thinking she was still in love with him. There's a ways to go in this story, but I promise you everything I've covered and I'm yet to cover is true.

I told her what was going on in my life and talked about my two kids. Then, I asked her why she hadn't contacted me when she got back to NY.

She said the obvious, "You're married." Then she added that I it was best that she stayed away from me.

At one point, I looked straight at her and asked her if she had been pregnant with our baby in June 1976. She said no. I had to take her word for it. There had been no confirmation or hint to her being pregnant aside from her saying she might have been.

We were there for a couple of hours and got caught up on things. After everything we'd been through together over the past eleven years, there was an easiness and a comfort level there for both of us. It was as if the nearly three and a half years that we hadn't seen each other never happened.

Over the next few months, I didn't contact her. I'd thought about what she said about it being best that she stay away from me. By about May, I just had to drop in on her though. She was working again at the same place she was at before she left for Florida. I saw her a few times over the next few months, always at her job.

Like I said earlier in the story, there was nothing at all going on between us physically, but there still seemed to be that underlying, unsaid emotional connection. In mid-August, we got together for drinks, and she once again had some news for me.

Take a guess.

This time, she'd met a guy who was in the military. She was going to marry him and move to California. This was a re-run of what happened in '83, and yes, once again, I felt that she was trying to get away from me so as not to break up my marriage.

Go on. Say it. *Conceited, a lousy husband,* and probably a bunch of other things that I won't even begin to mention. That's okay. Think of me what you will. You'd be right about at least some of it.

I was shocked that she was going to not only get married again, but that she was leaving NY again. I didn't say anything about it when she told me her plans, but I decided right then and there that I wasn't going to let her go away again.

For some reason, I felt that if she left this time that I would never ever see her again, I wasn't about to let that happen.

A couple of days later, I called her and told her I wanted to take her somewhere that I'd always wanted to go with her, but we'd never been. I told her it would be a nice way to say goodbye. She agreed, and in late August, we spent an afternoon at a local amusement park.

We went on the rides, shot water into the clown's mouth to make the balloon on his head fill with water and burst, had some carney food and a few drinks. It was a nice afternoon. It was getting to be time to head home, but before we did, I asked her to take a walk on the boardwalk with me.

We came to a bench overlooking the beach where we sat down and talked for a few minutes about her upcoming plans. Then I told her I didn't want her to go, I was still in love with her, and I felt if she did this I'd never see her again. I told her I'd do anything and everything that had to be done so we could be married.

She responded with the obvious response, "But Mike, you're married, and you have kids now, and I promised I was going to marry him." Then she said something that I'll never forget. She said, "Those should have been my kids."

I didn't respond to that comment, but I thought, she's right. They should have been her kids. We should have been married a long time ago, and she, Luca, Jeannette, and I should have been a family.

I just looked at her for a few seconds and told her I understood. Then I said, "I have one more thing to ask of you. Will you marry me someday?"

Without any hesitation she said, "Yes, I'll marry you some-day…when the time is right."

I said, "Okay, when the time is right, we'll get married."

She was sitting on my right, so I held out my right hand with my pinkie extended. She looked at me and wasn't sure what to do. I told her to give me her left hand and to extend her pinkie, so she did. I wrapped my pinkie around hers, and it was a done deal. Our promise was sealed with a pinkie promise, and we all know how serious a pinkie promise is!

We smiled at each other and got up from the bench. We didn't say much on our walk to my car, but finally having agreed to get married (someday) seemed to make both of us very happy. That was the fifth time in eleven years that the subject of marriage came up between us. Then, I took her home. I declined the invitation to her wedding. I had a wife and two little kids that were my priority. Zorina got married two weeks later, and I was sure that I would never see her again.

Neither of us had ever let go of the other. Neither one of us ever could. After eleven years and being married to other people, we made a promise to marry each other someday when the time was right. The door between us remained open as it always had been.

It didn't take long for me to start feeling the loss of her again. I wrote two more poems.

What Is True

Why do you keep running
Whenever I want you near
Another one to marry
No love to share you hear

One thousand miles didn't do it
What makes you think three thousand will
New places, new faces that's alright
But it's me that you love still

Who we fooling here anyway
We both know what is true
Ain't nothing stronger than our love
The love between me and you

Deep down inside we know it
No one else can fill our hearts

So come on back to me babe
Please don't keep us apart

One day you'll look around
And find what I say is true
Ain't nothing stronger than our love
The love between me and you

Just remember on that day
That I always have loved you

Someday

Listening to you
So confused and crying
I hear what you're saying
But we both know you're lying

How can you leave
Knowing you love me
To exist with another
You're just running away

And the game goes on
As it has for so long
Remembering what love was
From the radio's songs

Tender those days were
So fragile like you
Then broken and shattered
My fault and yours too

You told me "Someday"
But now I know better
Your leaving this time
Is leaving forever

I got a letter from Z in October letting me know how things were going with her. Here's part of what she wrote dated 10/22/87.

I do miss my friends over there sometimes, but being with Juan makes up for it. You can't imagine how much I love him. He makes me very happy. He is everything I ever dreamed of. Believe me I can't complain about anything. Give my love to Anna Lee and the kids. Take care and don't work too hard. Until we hear from you.

Zorina

Life went on. I didn't go into a downward spiral this time. I knew where Zorina was and could contact her at any time. She seemed very happy, and I was happy for her. I hoped that her new life in California was going to be what she'd been searching for.

We got a Christmas card from Z and Juan in '87. She had asked that if we were to go to California to please try and visit them. I had relatives out there, but we didn't have any plans to head out that way. It had to be sometime in late February that she contacted me and said she would be in NY for a visit to see her kids by mid-March.

Knowing I would be seeing her soon, I wrote this on March 4th, 1988.

Do not forsake he who was a boy
And who acted as one
Rather, love him for the man that he has become
For he is love…
With no beginning and no end

I saw Zorina on March 13th. I have a dated photo that she took of me that day. I met Z at her daughter's apartment. I was very surprised to see that Z was about five months pregnant!

Z and I went out for a while for a bite to eat and caught up on life, then we went back to the apartment. Zorina's daughter, Jeannette, had two kids by this time. So, at the age of thirty-nine, Z was a grandma, twice over, and she was having a baby!

Jeannette and a friend were going to go do some shopping, so Zorina and I had Jeannette's kids to watch for a while. We took them down the block to a small park that had some swings, a slide, and some benches to sit on. It was so good to see her, since I'd thought I never would again after we went to that amusement park.

Our lives had gone in such different directions. The photo she had taken of me was me pushing Jeannette's two kids, Zumo (age six months), and "Little Zorina" (age two and a half) on the swings. Many years later, that photo would come in handy for me.

Jeannette and her friend returned, and it was time for me to head home. Zorina and I gave each other a hug and said our goodbyes. Again, I had that impending feeling that I would never see her again. In late March, she sent a letter to us thanking me for taking her out that afternoon.

She wrote:

I am hoping, you may say planning, to go back to NY in September, but whenever I do go, I'll give you a call. Maybe we'll be able to get together. Well Mike, take care of yourself. Hopefully, I'll see you soon. Don't forget you have a good friend in California that wishes you and your loved ones a great and wonderful time at Easter.

Happy Easter.
Love, Zorina

I was doing okay after I saw her, but her being pregnant surprised me. It was hard to imagine that at her age she was going to have another child. Having seen her and finding out what was going on in her life moved me to write again.

The Rose

Picked a rose so long ago
Thought it was right to let it go
Loved that rose with all my heart
Realized we shouldn't be apart

But the thorns have gotten in my way
Each time I try and so I pray
I love that rose want to hold it near
To love it always and stop my tears

I still had her in my heart, but she was someone else's wife and pregnant, and I was someone else's husband with two small kids. I was doing okay, but at the same time, I was grappling with the situation. In that letter, Zorina said she hoped to be back to visit by September which made that a couple of months after her baby was born.

In June, I received a birthday card from her that stated she was planning on being back in NY within a couple of weeks, and she would let me know if she made the trip. I wasn't sure why she might be back so soon. As it turned out, I didn't hear from her. As far as I knew, she didn't make the trip. She signed off in that card she sent me with this:

MICHAEL AVELLINO

My dear Mike,

I hope to God that you have a wonderful Birthday. Have many, many more. And may God bless you today on your birthday and every day of your life.

Love You, Zorina

Unforeseen things were about to happen in my life that would eventually bring to fruition my greatest fear.

Chapter Nine

About a month later, Anna Lee and I found out that a couple of departments from our company were planning to relocate to another state. Anna Lee was in one of those departments. Nobody had to go, but if you were interested, it would be all expenses paid for the move.

In NY, we had a nice house. Both of our families were within an hour of us. The kids were both still too young for school, and both of our jobs were not the normal 8-5, Monday through Friday.

I was on rotational shifts, and weekends about every six weeks, and she would sometimes have to stay late or even go in to work in the middle of the night on an emergency basis. This was back in the stone age when there wasn't any internet yet, so working from home for her was not an option, and my job required me to be on the road. A move to another state would impact us, especially with our kids being so young.

I was against the move, but she wanted to go and was insisting on it. Finally, by late August, she drew a line in the sand. She was going and taking the kids, and I could stay in NY. To keep the peace, I agreed to go too. I had a very, very bad feeling about the whole thing, but off we went by early October.

In early September I called Zorina to let her know what was happening. It was a short and quick call. I didn't have any forwarding address info since we didn't know where we'd be living yet, and there were no cell phones or email. Stone age days, remember? I didn't even think to ask her about her baby, since I was in such a hurry.

September was a scramble to get ready to move. Our families weren't that hot on the idea either, especially our parents. They wouldn't be seeing their grandkids for a while or very often for that matter. We got moved, got a house, were unpacking, running the kids to day care, dealing with our jobs, and learning a new town/area. To say the least, it was very overwhelming.

We made it through Christmas and through that winter, but the strain was starting to wear us a bit thin, coupled with the fact that I didn't want to be there in the first place. I'm an easy-going guy, but at some point, if you push the wrong button with me, there's no undoing the damage. It was just a matter of time before that button was pushed.

I hadn't contacted Zorina to let her know where I was. She had no way to contact me, and I was putting off contacting her. I had seen her when she was pregnant. She seemed very happy with her marriage, and she had a new life in California. I knew where she was and felt it was best to maybe let things go for a while until I could see where things were headed on my end.

Having no contact with her, by September of '89, I began what would be my third downward spiral. I didn't want to go home after work, I didn't want to be where I was, no extended family, no familiar surroundings. I was living a life that I didn't want in any shape or form.

By early October, I was a mental mess. I wanted out, but I was stuck someplace I didn't want to be, in a situation that I didn't want to be in. That's when I wrote the following:

The Halls of Your Mind

In the halls of your mind
Lay the secrets of your past
Echo's in those halls
That you wish wouldn't last

Wake up in the morning
In a cold, cold sweat
Wake up seeing ghosts
You haven't even met
You want to see the sun

And the waking hours bring you
Even much more pain
The sunshine that you wanted
Has only turned to rain
So you wait for the night

Again in the halls of your mind
Lay the secrets of your past
Echo's in your halls
That you wish wouldn't last

Give me the night
Give me the night

I was on edge again. I didn't want to see tomorrow. My marriage was on its last leg, and I had no one to turn to, no one that I could sit down with and just let it out.

Going into December, things had fallen apart at home with Anna Lee. One evening, she handed me divorce papers. She'd already been to an attorney and started the process. She'd never said anything about getting a divorce, although things had not been good at all with us for a few months. I was somewhat relieved she'd done it, but at the same time, that was the button that got pushed that, for me, there was no going back.

She was a good wife and a good mother to the kids, but she was head strong, and she would make decisions that affected me without conferring with me. This was one time that I was all for giving her what she wanted. We'd have to sell the house and get places of our own.

The only thing I told her was this, "Whatever you do, don't take the kids and go back to NY, and leave me here. I came out here at your request. I didn't want to be here."

I tried to call Zorina. I just wanted to talk to her, tell her what was going on in my life, ask her about the baby, and how things were going for her, but to my unpleasant surprise, her phone had been disconnected. I'd waited too long to contact her, and she didn't know how to reach me.

I figured that since she was married to a soldier, he'd been reassigned somewhere and that she and the baby went with him. Somewhere could be anywhere. I didn't know where she was, and it was eating away at me.

For the second time in my life, I had no way to contact her. It had been sixteen months since we last spoke to each other on the phone, and now between her move to the west coast and my move out of NY, we'd lost touch. I thought of her often, very often, but we didn't even have any common friends any more that I could call. I had a phone number for her daughter in NY, but I didn't realize/remember that I had it. It was in one of the letters she had written to me and those were in that box of mementos I had, but I would only add things to that box and not normally read what was already in there.

Chapter Ten

A co-worker of mine asked me if I was interested in meeting someone. Stu was a good friend, a drinking and softball buddy. I'd shared what was going on in my marriage with him, so he knew I was on my way to being single. He was dating someone, and a friend of hers had seen me, and was interested in meeting me. Her name was Diane. When Stu told me about her, I knew who he was talking about, but I didn't even know her name. I figured, what the hell, so the four of us got together for drinks one evening.

Diane and I hit it off immediately. My divorce was started, I was moving into an apartment, and I was dating Diane. The only problem was that I wanted to get back to NY. It was January '90, and my life was very unstable. I like stability. I'm not one for turning my life or someone else's life upside down to see if making a certain choice would maybe be a good idea. To me that's just craziness.

The divorce was proceeding, I'd moved into an apartment, and I was seeing Diane a couple of days a week. As upside down as things were for me, I was pretty happy with the way things were going with her.

By early April, the house sold and that's when I found out Anna Lee was packing it all up and heading back to NY. I was livid…to a point. I'd never imagined that Diane and I would be so good together. So, here I was in the midst of a divorce, living on my own, and I had a girl in my life that was fantastic. I was going to put in for a transfer back to NY, but as the weeks went by, I delayed on placing that request.

I had to give things a chance with Diane. It was just too good to walk away from it. In about six months, Diane and I got a place together. The divorce was still lingering, and my hopes of moving back east were fading quickly. About a year after my divorce was finalized, I asked Diane to marry me. I wanted to tell Zorina, but I didn't know where she was. I felt so strongly about letting her know about Diane, and that I was doing okay that I wrote her a letter that I knew I couldn't send anywhere.

It's dated April 13th, 1993. I still have that letter. Here is some of what I wrote:

Zorina,

Hello, I hope you are well. I have been doing very well considering some of what is going on in my life right now. I've been apart from my wife Anna Lee for three years now. I don't know where you are or how to reach you. I met someone very special just after Anna Lee and I separated three years ago. Her name is Diane and she saved me from myself. I've asked her to be my wife. When we first met, she asked me how I could be so sure of our being right for one another. I told her about my relationship with you.

You will always be very special to me. The person I am today, you made me. I am today who I am and what I am mostly due to you. And I thank you for it. You allowed me to see things as they can be rather than as they actually are. I hope you too have found that happiness again. You deserve it more than anyone I know.

Michael

I showed the letter to Diane to let her know how much she (Diane) meant to me. Then, I put the letter away with the other things that I had kept from my time with Zorina. With the divorce finalized, Diane and I were married. She didn't want kids, and I already had two, so we were okay with not having any of our own. We were very happy together, and I didn't end up moving back to NY.

Her family became my family. Her parents were very good people and treated me very well. My kids would come out to visit a few weeks a year, and I'd get to NY and see them, the rest of my relatives, and friends every couple of years.

I would think of Zorina very often, but our lives had gone separate ways. I always thought of her on her birthday and on March 5th, the date we considered to be our anniversary. I wondered what happened to her, and I'd pray that she was okay and doing well.

Diane and I were doing great. We made a life together and were very happy. I met my buddy Ray a couple of years after Diane and I met. He had been dating a friend of hers for a while, and we hit it off and became very good friends. We're both former NY'ers so we had lots to talk about, especially since we're both baseball fans. Ray eventually met Irene who would become his wife, and the four of us did lots of things together over the years.

My buddy Stu and I had drifted apart at this point since the new job I had at our company was in a different location than where he was. We'd see each other once in a while and stop and say hello, but our lives had gone in different directions. It would be many years before Stu and I reconnected and had a close friendship again.

By the year 2000 my company began laying people off who were nearing full retirement. I got caught in that situation in 2003. For the next four years, I tried different types of work and couldn't find my niche, plus I wasn't making anywhere near the money I had been making before. This would cause a problem in our marriage.

We were struggling a bit financially, and Diane was feeling the strain. This went on for a couple of years, until I finally got a more stable job with a computer/printer company. It was still only about 60% of what I had been making in 2003, but it was steady work.

In July 2008, Diane and I went to NY for a week to visit my family. One day, we were at my parents' place, and I don't know how, why, or what prompted my dad to say this, but I think it was just to draw a comparison to Diane who is about 5'8" and blonde.

He said, "When Mike was younger, he seemed to date shorter, dark-haired girls. There was one he dated, and she was a very beautiful girl. I saw her one time."

Diane and I both knew that he was talking about Zorina. It was the only time in thirty-two years that he ever mentioned Z. I didn't say anything when he mentioned her, but it made me feel good that he had made a compliment about her.

I wish Dad would have been more of a "Ward Cleaver" type, but he didn't like the situation I would have been in with Z. It wasn't anything against Zorina personally, he just didn't want me to get in over my head with her, but then he never knew how much we loved each other as different as we were.

The financial crisis of 2008 hit. Over the next seven years, I would get laid off and re-hired four times at the printer company. In 2015 our department was being relocated to Georgia, so anybody who didn't or couldn't make that move was let go, including me. This caused a problem again in our marriage.

By early 2016, I was working part time and taking care of most of the house and home responsibilities. The business I was working for was in town just a few miles away. It was at this point that I met my future friend, Kay. She worked for another business in town. I didn't know her name or anything about her, but about every couple of weeks, I had to get some paperwork signed off by her for my company. She'd always just scribble her signature, so it was pretty hard to read, but I could see that her first name was probably Kay.

I'd go into her office area and sometimes, I'd have to wait for her to finish up on the phone, or she'd be dealing with a co-worker in her office. We'd just say *hi*, she'd sign the paperwork, then I'd be on my way.

I have to say, for whatever reason, and I couldn't figure this out, she was kind of mesmerizing to me. Okay, so she's thin, very pretty, dark complexion, dark eyes, dark hair…I know what you're thinking…just my type!

Yes, but there was way more to it than that. Her look and the way she dressed were very attractive, but my attention was more focused on the way she talked to and dealt with people on the phone and her co-workers in her office. There was a familiarity there for me for some reason. I did think that if I wasn't married and very happily so, that I'd be all about her. I had some preconceived notions about her that I can say were about 95% accurate after I got to know her. When I watched her work and deal with people, it was kind of like watching a magician.

That would go on like that for about ten months. Finally, I said more than "thanks" for her signing the paperwork I had. I'll get back to her in a few minutes.

That summer, I ran into Stu at a gas station in town. He'd just moved there a few months before. We started up our friendship again, and it was nice to do some things together again.

By November, I began to notice something different going on with Diane. She was spending a lot of time on her cell phone at home both texting and talking, especially when she was out in the yard. It didn't give me a good feeling.

After some snooping on my part, I realized there was something going on with her. By early December, I confronted her, and she admitted she was texting and talking to a guy that was just a "friend".

I told her any friend of hers was a friend of mine, let's all do lunch. It seems he didn't think that was such a good idea, as I had suspected.

I told her I wanted things with him to end immediately. She said okay, but as it turned out, she just kept doing what she was doing. So, for about six weeks I was dealing with this by myself.

I didn't want to confide in family or even friends about it. I was too embarrassed, and I wanted to protect her reputation. I was beginning to lose my patience and my mind as well. I needed someone to talk to just to let it out, but I didn't want it to be anybody who was close to us.

A few days before Christmas, I went in to get some paperwork signed off by Kay. My head was spinning at this point about my marriage falling apart. She signed the paperwork, I said thanks and turned to head out the door.

Then she said, "And you have a very Merry Christmas."

I stopped and said, "And you have a very Merry Christmas too."

Before I pushed that door open to leave, I'd made up my mind…it was her. She was the one I was going to ask to get together to talk to. Those few kind words of hers, wishing me a Merry Christmas meant the world to me right at that point in time. I still couldn't figure out what it was about her that held my attention. Yeah, she was a good-looking woman and had this awesome way about her, but there was more to it. It was like I knew her, only I'd never met her before I had to do business with her over the last ten months or so.

Anyway, it was about three weeks later that I went to get some paperwork signed by her again. She was in the office by herself.

She signed off, and then I said, "Do you mind if I ask you a personal question?"

She said okay. I asked her if she was with someone, had someone in her life.

She said, "No. As a matter of fact, I just got off the phone with my lawyer. I'm in the process of a divorce."

I told her I was married, but that I was having marital problems, and I showed her the ring on my finger. I asked her if she would be open to getting together sometime for a drink or a cup of coffee, so I could pick her brain a bit about the court process. I told her how I didn't want to let family or friends know what was going on.

She kind of looked at me for a couple of seconds with her head cocked to one side as if she was wondering if I was asking her out, then she threw both hands into the air and said, "Sure. Why not?"

She gave me her number, and we got together a few days later. I told Diane about meeting with Kay, so she would know that I just needed to talk to somebody to clear my head.

It was January 2017, and over the next four weeks or so, we got together on Friday evenings for an hour or two each time. We never went anywhere together. We'd always meet at a restaurant and then go our own separate ways. For someone who grew up in what used to be a small town at the foot of the Rocky Mountains, Kay is very street smart, more like what I'd expect from a big city girl.

We had a good rapport, and as much as she was an outlet for me to talk to, I was an outlet for her as well. I'd tell her what was going on in my life, and she'd tell me about hers. She was very helpful with how the court process worked.

We could and would talk about everything and anything. I even mentioned Shakespeare's quote to her a couple of times, and we shared some stories about odd happenings we'd both experienced in the past.

In bits and pieces, I filled her in on what I was able to find out about Diane's "friend". A couple of weeks went by, and we met for lunch on a Saturday.

We were finishing up with lunch, and she said to me, "Tell me everything you know about this guy at one time right now."

So, I gave her the rundown. I knew his initials, what type of work he did, what town he lived in, and some of his extracurricular activities (besides my wife that is!).

She looked on her cell phone for about a minute and told me she thought she knew who he was. Yeah, I had the same reaction you just had.

I sat there for a few seconds, and said, "How can you possibly know who this guy is?"

She pulled a profile up on her phone and read through all the details online, and they matched everything I'd told her. She told me she was from the same town as him, and that they'd been classmates from junior high through high school. She gave me the name of who she thought it was.

So, let's back up about eleven months and recap this order of events. I'm mesmerized by this woman that I don't know, there's something about her that's very familiar, my marriage is in trouble, she wishes me a Merry Christmas, I ask her to get together for a drink, she says yes, and six weeks later tells me she thinks she knows who this guy is.

So, I told Kay, "If you're right, it's like a million to one shot that I approached you and you know who he is!"

She was like, "Yeah…that would be quite a coincidence."

Oh…there are more coincidences though.

I went home after lunch and asked Diane if this was the guy's name.

She looked at me and said, "I wish you wouldn't be searching online to find out who he is. He's just a friend."

When I told her how I got the name, she looked at me and said, "Really? This woman you've known for about a month told you?"

I said, "Yeah. All you have to do is ask him if he knows who she is."

The next day, Diane told me, "He knows who Kay is." Diane said, "That's like a million to one shot!"

I said, "Yeah, it is. Isn't it?"

Kay's divorce got finalized a couple of weeks later, and she was very adamant that she did not want a guy in her life. Her ex was a domineering type. He'd tell her how he wanted her hair to be cut and what type of clothes she could wear. So, as soon as she separated from him, she started wearing what she wanted and grew her hair out. She even had purplish highlights put in. She was free to be who she wanted to be, and she was loving every minute of it!

I think the most important point that Kay made to me, and it really resonated with me, was this—that I needed to try to put my emotions aside with the way I was approaching what was going on in my marriage and just look at the facts of what was actually happening and going on. That helped me to see things more clearly, without what I will call, the *emotional fog* that was influencing my decisions.

Over the next six months, we weren't getting together as often as we had been. There were at least one-month breaks. I needed to have someone a bit more accessible to talk to, but who?

There was another account that I had at work. I'd be in there up to three times a day five days a week. The woman who worked the counter was very nice. Kristine was always smiling, and she was always in a good mood. I'd been dealing with that account for about two months, and one day I went in there, and she was a bit down.

I asked her if she was doing okay. We always talked a lot, but we'd never talked about personal things. She said she and her boyfriend were splitting up. They'd been together for a long time. I told her I was going through the same type of thing in my marriage, and if she wanted to talk about things with me once in a while, it might be good for both of us. I told her how I had been doing that with a new friend named Kay for the last few months.

Kristine thought it was a good idea, so whenever I went in there and there wasn't anybody else at the counter, we'd talk a bit about our relationship problems. I decided to expand my "female" base of people I could talk to, so I let Dee, who cut my hair, in on what was happening in my marriage. Dee knew Diane before she knew me, but Diane stopped getting her hair done by Dee about five years earlier.

I know…you're wondering what all this business has to do with Zorina. Remember, I mentioned "coincidences" and "statistical improbabilities" and what Zorina had written to me in the letter she sent me after she got out of the hospital in June '76, and Shakespeare's quote, and your own personal beliefs. This all ties together eventually.

Chapter Eleven

So, I had three people that I was confiding in—Kay, Kristine, and Dee. It was only those three and no one else.

About another month went by, and one day I was at Kristine's business waiting for the things I needed, and we got talking a bit again. On this day, I gave her just a bit more info about Kay than she'd known before.

Kristine looked at me and said, "Oh, I know Kay."

I sat there for a few seconds, and she was waiting for my response. I said, "Look, don't do that. It's not funny. There's already a few coincidences involving Kay and my life that are kind of astronomically improbable."

She said, "No, really. I know Kay. We're good friends."

Once again, I said, "That's not funny."

Then, she said, "We were going to get an apartment together, but the timing was off on our relationships breaking up. We did a lot of business with her and her ex-husband's business."

I had confided in two different (I thought), disassociated women only to find out they were friends. I mean what are the odds? I finally told all three women about the others that I had confided in soon after Kristine had told me she knew Kay. Maybe you're thinking these three women lived in close proximity to one another. Well, they didn't. They lived anywhere from twenty-five to forty miles apart and in different towns.

Kay and I were still getting together every month or so. I'd tell her she was my "Happy Pill". Whenever I saw her, even though it was for just an hour or two, I'd feel great, and at least for a while, my problems just didn't seem important anymore. Kay had a way of making me feel really good, as if I popped a "Happy Pill".

Truth be told, I was very much in love with my wife, and I was fighting desperately to save my marriage, but at the same time there was something about Kay that I still couldn't figure out, and I was kind of falling for her. I liked the way she saw the world and how she responded to it and to the people around her. I wrote a poem about her around mid-2017 that really just spoke about our friendship and what had gone on between us since we first got together for drinks in January. This is what I wrote:

Just Friends

She wished me a Merry Christmas
And those kind words made me smile
I'd thought about her in the past
But it had been quite a while

Then there was the moment
When I asked her if she could
Meet me for a drink or two
And she said that she would

I said I like your smile
And I like your style too
I told her of my problems
And she said she had some too

She led me through the darkness
Through the cold and callous night
To a place that was much safer
Where we both could see the light

And now there is a friendship
That I hold so very dear
We understand each other well
And she's helped me face my fears

Soon I hope to let her know
What I have inside of me
So she can let her guard down
Knowing well she'll still be free

July 7, 2017

We'd gotten together over a dozen times since January, and neither one of us had ever run into anyone we knew. It was over Labor Day weekend that we met for breakfast. The place was very busy, and on this day, we took a bit longer than we normally did for a meal. We'd been there for two and a half hours.

She needed to use the restroom before we left, and I was at our table paying the check. I looked up from the table, and I literally started to shake a bit. Dee and a couple of other people were being seated a few tables away.

When Kay got back, I said, "You remember I told you about Dee who cuts my hair and she's the third and last person I've confided in about my marriage?"

She said, "Yeah."

I said, "Dee just got seated over there. Would you mind saying hello to her, since I've told her about you?"

She was okay with that, so I introduced them. They gave each other a hug, and they talked for a minute. Once again…what are the odds?

There had been a string of coincidences in about a nine-month time frame, and they were all related to what was going on with my marriage. Each one individually seemed statistically improbable, but when you string them all together, they became astronomically improbable.

Diane and I had officially filed the court papers at the end of August '17. She didn't want the divorce. She wanted me and our family life together and her "friend" as well on the side. She let me know that I could have "female friends" if I wanted.

I advised her that a marriage was a partnership between two

people, and it didn't include a silent partner on the side. I was done with the whole thing.

I told her, "You want him? You got him."

Diane had been the beneficiary of what I'd wanted to give of myself to Zorina years earlier, but in her mind, it was now the 21st century and those Neanderthal ideas of one man with one woman were outdated. It could be ninety days or slightly longer to get things finalized.

In September, we began telling our friends and relatives that we were splitting up. It came as a surprise to all of them. When I told Ray and his wife Irene, she began crying just a bit and gave me a hug. I gave them a rundown on everything that had gone on over the last year, including how and why I approached Kay, and all the coincidences.

When I mentioned Kristine, Ray said, "Oh, I know Kristine."

I sat there for a few seconds, figuring he was just messing with me. I said, "Okay, now don't even go there."

He said, "No, really. I know Kristine. I've dealt with her through my business."

Sure enough, he knew who she was. Just another one of those silly "coincidences."

In late 2017, both Ray and Stu were keeping closer tabs on me. They were concerned about me due to the divorce. I was really doing okay at that point, but their friendships helped keep things on an even keel for me. During that holiday season, I would start spending my time with them and their families, since I had no family close by and my divorce was nearly finalized.

It was early November 2017, and Kay and I got together for a bite to eat one evening to celebrate her birthday. I liked to tease Kay once in a while just to get a reaction out of her. Months earlier, for some reason, the subject of women's underwear, in particular "thongs", came up. I'd remembered that conversation, so I gave her a small box that was wrapped with birthday paper and told her I had gotten her a pair of thongs for her birthday.

I could tell by her demeanor that she wasn't quite sure what to say or do. I was trying to keep from laughing out loud. She began to peel the paper off the box very slowly like she was peeling an artichoke. She was taking her time, since she was probably mortified that I'd bought her underwear. She was being so careful with it as well, like she was defusing a bomb that might explode at any second. She finally opened the box and had a bit of a stunned look on her face, and then she smiled.

She pulled the pair of thongs out of the box and started laughing. The pair of thongs that I'd gotten her weren't underwear, they were a novelty item—mini beach style rubber thongs that were made to put on the base of stemmed wine glasses.

She tried to get a wine glass from the waitress, but the place we were at didn't have any stemmed wine glasses. Having watched her agonize over opening her gift and her eventual reaction was kind of fun…for me that is! That evening was the first time that I told her that she was like an "angel on my shoulder." A couple of days later, I wrote a short poem about her.

Angels

You're an Angel on my shoulder girl
Keeping me safe in my crazy world
I love it when you laugh and smile
Though we're together for only a little while

Nov 15, 2017

It was the Saturday after Thanksgiving that I got a text from Kay just saying *hi*. It was very unusual that I'd hear from her on a weekend, unless we'd already made plans to get together. I texted her that I had a warm fire and a cold beer for her if she wanted to stop by. She didn't accept, and I wasn't surprised by her response. We texted for about an hour, then we agreed to get together again soon.

For some reason, I had an itch to watch the movie "The Good, The Bad, and The Ugly." I had the DVD, so I popped it in. One of the main character's names in the movie was "Angel Eyes." It reminded of what I had written recently about Kay being an *angel on my shoulder*, so I took about a twenty-minute break from the movie and wrote this:

Lone Rider

Lone Rider riding tired and slow
Riding long no place to go
Went down this road long time ago
Riding long no place to go

Lone Rider's facing it again
Like long ago remembering when
He hoped for someone just a friend
To help him get around the bend

And then an Angel soon appeared
To see him through and wrest his fears
That Angel helped to stop his tears
Lone Rider soon saw his way clear

The Angel and Lone Rider now
Helping each other find somehow
A lasting friendship that may allow
Them both to heal someway, somehow

Nov 25, 2017

Kay had been a very important and helpful friend for nearly a year. I wasn't sure why I'd singled her out, but something in me said she's the one I need to have in my life to help me right now. That's why I approached her when I did.

In "Lone Rider" I write, "went down this road long time ago", and "Lone Rider's facing it again like long ago remembering when." Both of those lines are referring directly to my relationship with Zorina, when we stopped seeing each other in late '76.

Kay, the "Angel", was helping me see my way clear during my divorce from Diane. Her friendship and moral support had kept me going. There had been a trust and some type of bond there for me with her. It would be about another eighteen months before I'd figure out what it was about Kay that affected me in such a positive way.

Diane and I had been together for nearly twenty-eight years, and we were always good and kind to one another, but the relationship had run its course. By late January '18, it was finished. About a month later, I went on a dating website and was ready to move on. I dated fifteen women over the next twelve months, and one of them I dated exclusively for four months. That one, Nicole, and I are still friends to this day. We still get together once in a while just as friends. Nicole, if she had wanted to, could have had me hook, line, and sinker. She has a big heart, a kind demeanor, a gentle soul, poise, elegance, grace, and a face that could launch a thousand ships. Need I say, this is one very exceptional woman.

I was having a good time and a couple of them really liked me, and I really liked a couple of them, but I just didn't click with the right one. Kay and I were still getting together every few months, and I'd hoped after my divorce was finalized that she might consider getting together as more than just friends.

One evening we were having a drink, and I looked at Kay and said, "I know I've asked you to get together for a concert or a movie sometime, and you've never accepted, but I feel like you're supposed to go do something with me even just as friends. This isn't just a line of BS I'm feeding you to get you to say okay. I really feel like we're supposed to go somewhere together sometime."

I really had been feeling that way, but I couldn't figure out why. Anyway, she still wouldn't take our relationship beyond a friendship.

New Year's 2018 going into 2019, I remember Ray and Irene asking me if I had any New Year's resolutions. I normally don't do that kind of thing.

In this instance, however, I said, "I'm going to make it to a beach this year."

It had been nearly twenty-five years since I'd been to the ocean. The last time was on my honeymoon with Diane in '94.

When early 2019 came around, I started planning a new home for myself. Diane and I had each done very well on the sale of our house. I was looking at getting a semi-custom built and was able to start planning it before they even broke ground, so I was able to get every option that I wanted in it.

There's a couple of smaller lakes and one fairly big lake a few miles long nearby. So, here's another one of those odd coincidences.

In one of my sit downs with the salesperson, we reviewed the available lots. The one I liked backed up to a road, but it was better than having neighbors behind you as well as neighbors very close on both sides of you. Besides, it was lot number-seven, the same number "The Mick" wore back in the day when he was the King of New York baseball! I signed all the necessary paperwork to get things started.

Then I asked, "By the way, what's the name of the street that lot is on?"

They said, "It's Sandy Beach Lake Lane." I nearly shit a pickle! So, the resolution I'd made a couple of weeks earlier to go to the beach was going to, in some capacity, come true. I'd be living on Sandy Beach Lake Lane.

My dating website subscription was up at the end of February, and I was debating whether I should extend it for another six months. Then, I thought to myself, I know what I like. I know what I want. I know what I'm looking for. I know who she is. I just need to find her.

On February 24th I cancelled my dating website subscription. I found a website that could locate people instead. It was a bit more expensive than most others, but it had very good reviews and could be cancelled at any time. It had been thirty-one years since we had seen each other, and over thirty years since we had any contact at all. I didn't know if she was married, or if she would still have me if she was single. I had to also consider the worst-case scenario—that she might not still be alive.

I embarked on a journey to fulfill a promise that we'd made to each other nearly thirty-two years earlier on that bench on the boardwalk at the amusement park. I began my search for Zorina.

Chapter Twelve

That afternoon I got signed up for the search website. I filled in the necessary info to find Zorina that they requested. The amount of information they provided out there was unbelievable. There were street addresses and phone numbers that I recognized for her that went back to the time we'd dated in '76. The most important piece of info I found was this—her age was current.

They had her listed as the age she should be. That told me she was still out there, that she was still alive. There were names of relatives, possible relatives, friends, their possible phone numbers, street addresses, and numerous email addresses for her as well. There was a lot to dig through. Day by day, I sent emails and called phone numbers. The website distinguished between land lines and cell phones.

I was going to be in NY in late September. My cousin James' son was getting married, so I would be attending the wedding. I began to think that once I found Zorina, we could talk and get reacquainted on the phone. If she was single, available, and interested, I could fly to NY just for a long weekend to see her by no later than April. I was moving into my house by June, so I'd be pretty settled in there by the time I went to NY, and if she wanted to, she could fly back with me and stay for a while.

During the first week of my search, I spoke to my buddy Ray and told him what I was doing. He had no knowledge of Zorina. He'd only known me since I was with Diane over the last twenty-seven years. I briefed him on some of my history with Z to explain why I was going to look for her. I got together with Stu one evening for a bite to eat and told him about my search as well. As I did with Ray, I explained to Stu some 'f my past relationship with Z, so he'd have a better understanding of why I was trying to find her.

About a week after I began my search for her, I'd narrowed things down quite a bit. Some of the email addresses that I'd sent emails to came back as *undeliverable*, but others went through, and yet I hadn't received a response.

I left a message at one land line, but no one called me back. Other phone numbers were disconnected. A couple of days later, I found a possible connection that also had a *Facebook* page referenced. I thought it might be Zorina's granddaughter, the one in the photo that Z had taken when we took her grandkids to the park in March of '88.

I searched the internet for what I thought was her grand-daughter's name and found a photograph of that girl with Zorina. It was a head shot of the two of them, dated as 2013, and Z's hair was blonde. I'd only known Z when her hair was naturally jet black, but it was her in that photograph.

It was now day-ten of my search. Since I was getting a bit frustrated with the emails and phone numbers, I decided to write Zorina a letter and mail it to one of two addresses that I'd narrowed things down to. Here is that letter:

Zorina,

March 5th, 2019

Hi. I hope this letter has made its way to you. I've tried to locate you on the internet, but I haven't had much luck, so I resorted to the old fashioned "write a letter and mail it" method since I just found two addresses out there. I'm trying this one first. I tried a few email addresses and phone #'s that I came across, but none of them panned out for me.

Zorina, I don't mean to interfere in your life in any way. It's been more than 30 years since we last saw and communicated with each other. I've thought of you often. So many times, I prayed to God that you were ok and doing well. I tried to locate you in the early '90's, but that was pre-internet. I think you went back to NY after living in CA and I couldn't locate you so I felt maybe I should just let things be. Now, these many years later, neither of us is getting any younger and recently I hoped maybe this might be the time to re-establish a dialogue between us.

How are you? What is your life like? Are you ok? Are you well? Are you _________? (fill in the blank!). Enclosed is a copy of a photo that you took of me in 1988. I think it may have been the last time that we saw each other. I hope that if you receive this letter, you will respond. I would like very much to hear from you.

Michael

I'd written the letter in the early evening hours of March 5th and planned to mail it the next day. That evening, between *Facebook* and the location website search, I found a phone number for the girl who I thought might be Z's granddaughter. It was listed as a cell phone number, so I sent a text.

Hi. My name is Michael. Are you also known as Little Zorina? If so, I dated your Grandma Zorina many years ago and I'm trying to find her.

This was the response I received:

Michael, is that you? I can't believe you still have my number.

I was a bit confused by the response, but at the same time, I was very excited. My mind began racing. Maybe it was Zorina, but I never had that phone number, there were no cell phones in the late '80's. Maybe her granddaughter had the phone in her own name, but it was Zorina's to use? I was so close. Was it Z, or was it Little Z who could give me the contact info I needed to call Zorina? I sent back a one-word text.

Zorina???

I received this response:

This is Little Zorina. My Grandma Zorina died a few years ago.

I froze.

The search website had shown what Zorina's current age would be. I was sure she was still alive, and now I received this text from her granddaughter.

I lowered myself to the floor. I sat with my back against the wall, held my head in my hands, and broke down.

A couple of minutes later I texted:

NO NO NO

Little Z: Yes. She died from liver cancer.

Me: Do you know who I am?

Little Z: Yes, you and my grandma dated when I was a teenager.

Me: No. I dated her in the mid '70's. I have a photo that she took of me pushing you in a swing when you were about 2 years old in 1988.

She asked that I text that photo to her, so I did.

Little Z: Oh, I'm sorry. Grandma dated someone else named Michael when I was in my teens. I thought you were him.

At this point, I was on an emotional roller coaster. I was confused, and I was hurting. Little Z texted me a photo of Zorina and something that Z had written in her last couple of weeks for her friends and family. This is just an excerpt from it:

When I leave you don't weep for me. Pass the wine around and remember how my laughing pleased you. Look at one another smiling and don't forget about touching. Sing the songs I loved best and dance one time all together. As for me, I'll be off, running somewhere on the beach. When you're ready I'll be there – waiting for you. Take your time.

Then I received another text from her:

My mom is very excited. She wants to talk to you.

Unbeknownst to me, while I was texting Little Z, she was texting her mom (Zorina's daughter, Jeannette), and Little Z had forwarded that photo I sent her to her mom. I was an emotional mess. I texted back that right now was not a good time for me to talk to her, that I was devastated by the news of Zorina's passing. A couple of minutes later I received another text.

Little Z: My mom says it's very important. She has something to tell you that my grandma told her about you.

I was in no condition to talk to anybody at that moment, but there was something very urgent that Jeannette wanted to tell me, so I texted Little Z to have her mom call me. I tried very quickly to get myself together so I could speak to her. A couple of minutes later, my phone rang, and I answered it.

Before I continue, I want to make my last "Acknowledgement" to this story. I want to thank Zorina's daughter, Jeannette, for her kindness, her hospitality, and her understanding. She's been like a daughter to me, and she's filled in a thirty-year gap in time with answers and information that is invaluable to me. The rest of this story could not have been written without the things she's shared with me.

Jeannette and I said hello, then I told her how sorry I was that her mom had passed away. She expressed that she was very glad to hear from me. I told her that today was the 43rd anniversary of my first date with her mom and how Z and I had met two days before that.

She gave me the details of Z's cancer, and how it didn't get discovered until it was in its final stages. From the time it was diagnosed, until Zorina passed away, was less than two months. In that time, she was seeing the doctors and entered the hospital for treatments, but there really wasn't much that could be done. The cancer had advanced too far.

When a liver fails, toxins in the body are not removed. This can cause numerous physical problems, as well as confusion and forgetfulness.

Jeannette went on to say this to me, "When Mom found out it was terminal cancer, she wanted to try to find you. She wanted to see you. We started to search, but she couldn't remember the exact spelling of your last name."

At that point, it had been twenty-six years since we'd had any contact, since the phone call I made to her in late '88 to tell her I was leaving NY. After all those years, she wanted to see me one last time to say goodbye. Zorina passed away in late October 2014 just four days shy of her 66th birthday.

I thanked Jeannette so much for letting me know that, after all those years, Zorina thought of me and wanted to see me. I told her I loved her mom very much, and I still loved her, and that's why I came looking for her. I told her I was so sorry for hurting her mom the way I did, that I didn't mean for it to be that way, that I thought it might be best for both of us if we stopped dating. I told Jeannette I was wrong, and that I just didn't understand what her mom was trying to convey to me.

Then Jeannette said, "But that's not what I wanted to tell you."

I thought, there's more?

Jeannette proceeded to tell me about a conversation they'd had. Jeannette used the term a "mother-daughter conversation". She said they spoke about Zorina's life, her childhood, her marriages, her children, friends, and events that had happened. Jeannette had asked her if there was any one guy in her life that was more special than the rest.

Jeannette said to me, "Michael…Mom said it was *you*. Mom said you were the love of her life. She had only very fond memories of you, and she had no regrets."

I was already an emotional train wreck from finding out Z had passed away, and now I broke down again on the phone. Again, I expressed how much I had loved and still did love Zorina. I told her that I always wanted to believe that was how her mom had always felt about me, that I'd hoped it wasn't just me, from my end, holding on to something inside of me that maybe wasn't really there anymore. I thanked her for letting me know that.

I went on to tell Jeannette that I'd be in NY in September, and if possible, I'd like to see her and Little Z. She was very open to that and said to plan on it when I was there.

I told her I wanted to visit Zorina's resting place. I assumed it was in NY, but she told me her mom was buried in her hometown in Puerto Rico…San Sebastian. That was the first time I'd ever heard the name of Z's hometown.

I mentioned to Jeannette that I had written some poetry about her mom years earlier and that I would send a few to her in an email. I just wanted her to know how deeply I felt about her mom. I explained to her that I never shared any of these poems with Zorina, she never saw any of them. I ended up emailing Jeannette "I Was", "Times", and "I Remember Yesterday" along with a copy of the letter that I was going to mail the next day that I'd written to send to Z. Jeannette and I would communicate through emails for the next seven months and we, along with Little Z, would meet in late September.

About a week after I found out that Zorina had passed away, I met Kay for an after-work bite to eat. I hadn't seen her or talked to her since November, four months earlier. I was very anxious to see her and tell her what was going on in my life.

She told me how her dog had just passed away and how she was dealing with that. I didn't mean to play "can you top this", but I told her about looking for Z and that we had dated decades ago.

I had never mentioned Zorina to Kay before by name, but I had made a couple of general references about her in our previous conversations. I didn't get into any deep details about Z except to say that we'd had a very serious relationship that didn't work out, and that we'd promised each other we'd get married someday.

Kay could tell that I was deeply affected by Z's passing. As I was talking, I had to stop a few times to take a breath. She'd never seen me like that. Not even when I was having marital problems with Diane. It was good to see her and have some time together to catch up on each other's lives. For the fourth time in my life, Zorina was going to consume my thoughts and my heart, and I had very little to no control over it.

The day after I saw Kay, I wrote the first poem about Zorina that I'd written in twenty-nine years. I was so emotionally charged that I had to put my thoughts on paper.

My Long Lost Love

Went searching for my long lost love
I searched and prayed to God above
That she was safe and doing well
My love for her I hoped to tell

Sweet memory that filled my dreams
She's been gone four years it seems
To find my love Zorina I tried
But now there's teardrops in my eyes

Then I was told how much she cared
About the love that we had shared
And though she'd never been my wife
I was the love of her life

I'll hold you in my heart my love
Till my time comes to fly above
In life you were out of my reach
But someday we'll meet on that beach

And there we'll love and laugh and play
We two forever and a day

I'll hold you near
I'll love you dear
And never let you go ever again…

March 11, 2019

I got an email from Jeannette saying that she thought the poems that I sent to her were beautiful, and that she'd like permission to print them out and place them in Zorina's "tomb." I happily agreed and let her know that I was humbled by her wanting to place them with her mom. I advised her that I had about a dozen poems, and that I'd print them out and mail them to her so she could place all of them at Z's resting place in Puerto Rico. She was okay with that.

I have to admit, that I had a bit more in mind when I told her I'd send the poetry. I ended up copying some of the cards and letters that Z had given me, as well as sending copies of photographs of us and some of the mementos I'd kept. It took me a couple of weeks to put that together. In all, there were about twenty pages that I put in a nice leather binder and mailed to her. Everything that Zorina and I had written to each other and about each other was all from the heart. I just wanted to give Jeannette a better idea of what her mom and I meant to each other in our own original words.

After I mailed that to Jeannette, I began to read all of Z's cards and letters in depth. I read them multiple times as well. Through April and into May, I kept re-reading them along with the poetry that I'd written about her. It inspired me to write the following:

My Rose of San Sebastian

My rose of San Sebastian
I miss you oh so much
Longing for your love again
Longing for your touch

Barefoot by the water
Will you hold me once again
Together on that sandy beach
Until I don't know when

My rose of San Sebastian
I'd like another chance
When my time comes to be with you
Can we please finish our dance

May 22, 2019

In those six weeks or so that I'd been reviewing everything that I'd kept from my relationship with Zorina, I figured out what it was about Kay that struck a chord with me. It had been over three years since I'd first met Kay, but I finally understood why I referred to her as my "Happy Pill" and as an "Angel on my shoulder". I knew at this point that getting together with her was about to end by my own choice.

Since that initial contact with Jeannette in early March through May, I was trying to deal with Zorina's passing. There were many times that I'd experience overwhelming moments of grief.

One evening in late April, my mom called me. She was frantic on the phone and kept asking me if I was okay. It took me about five minutes to calm her down and convince her that I was fine. I don't know what triggered that from her, but she'd never done that before.

We spoke for about fifteen minutes. It wasn't until we got off the phone that I wondered what caused her to be like that. I hadn't told anyone outside of Ray and Stu about having searched for Zorina, and they have no contact info for anyone back in NY related to me, so my mom had no knowledge of it. I wasn't going to tell her and my dad that I searched for Z until I could do it in person when I went to NY in September.

A couple of weeks later, I called my mom on Mother's Day. We spoke for a few minutes, then out of nowhere, she said to me that she'd heard that song on the radio, "You'll Never Find Another Love Like Mine" the day before.

She said, "You know, the song that Zorina dedicated to you."

I was stunned by what she'd just said to me. I didn't even remember telling her that forty-three years ago.

I said, "Mom, I told you about that?"

She said, "Yes, when you were dating her."

Once she brought up that subject, I just couldn't hold back. I told her about my search for Z, that she'd passed away, how she tried to find me, and that her daughter told me I had been the love of Zorina's life.

My mom began to cry. Here it was Mother's Day, and I made my mom cry on the phone. I told her I'd fill her in on everything when I came to NY.

Not long after that, I emailed Jeannette and told her how my mom had brought up the subject of Zorina. Jeannette stated that would have made Zorina very happy.

Then she wrote, "Honestly, part of Mom's pain was that she believed your family never felt she was good enough for you. It was only many years later that she came to understand their point of view."

I responded to the revelation that Jeannette had made.

It was my dad looking out for me. It was the situation. It wasn't your mom personally that concerned him.

I also stated, *Neither of us ever did anything to intentionally hurt the other. When there's a lot of love, there can be a lot of pain as well as unintentional as it might be.*

I finished up by writing, *there were so many good and fun times Zorina and I had together, and the love was always there, and it's still there, and it always will be.*

I closed on my new home in early May and moved into it in early June. It was a very hectic time for me. I wanted to see Kay to tell her what I realized about her, but finding the time to get together was a bit of a challenge. We finally got together for lunch in early July.

As always, it was good to see her, but after what I was going to say to her, I felt that it was probably best for me to not see her again. We talked for a while, and she got me up to date with what was going on with her.

Then I said, "Kay, I've had an epiphany, and it involves you."

She looked at me, and her eyes opened wide. She had a bit of a stunned look on her face, but at the same time she was like, "Okay. Okay, tell me. Tell me."

I said, "Do you remember how over the last couple of years I kept asking you to go out with me, but that I couldn't figure out why it seemed so important, and how you always make me feel so good just talking to you, and you're my Happy Pill and an Angel on my shoulder?"

In a half questioning way she said, "Yeah."

I said, "Here's why. Do you remember I told you about how I went looking for Zorina, but she passed away? Well, I went through her cards and letters numerous times that she had given me, and I began to remember who she was, and what she was… her way about her, and how she dealt with people. The two of you are very different people with your likes and dislikes, although you both have a similar look and style, but it goes beyond that. What I realized is that your personalities are basically one in the same. As far as personality goes, I see her in you. I just never made the connection until recently."

Kay said, "Well, she must have been a lot of fun!"

That made me smile, and I acknowledged that yes, Z was lots of fun to be with!

Then I said, "Remember a couple of years ago, I spoke about Shakespeare's quote from Hamlet: '*There are more things in Heaven and earth Horatio, than are dreamt of in your philosophy*', and that I always took that line to mean that there may be energies, entities, spirits, guardian angels, you know…the kinds of things that go beyond what we can see and touch or even understand?"

I handed Kay part of the letter that Z had written to me after she got out of the hospital in'76. I told her to read that one paragraph that said:

> *If you ever need anybody to talk to or you need a friend around remember what I always told you. You will always have a friend in me, and I will never let you down. So, when your pretty eyes are full with tears or the sound of this cruel world is driving you crazy baby, don't worry. I will always be there and try to make things right for you.*
> *So, when you feel like crying and there is no one who has the time to sit and ask you why… when you need someone to hear you or just be near you baby, I will be close by and you can come to talk to me as a friend.*
> *My love will always be with you.   Z*

I said to Kay, "Okay, now just play along here for a minute. Z passed away at the end of 2014. I first saw you in early 2016, although we didn't get together for drinks until early 2017. What if, just what if…Shakespeare's quote is true? What if something or someone, maybe Zorina, who couldn't physically be here for me, brought you into my life to help me get through my breakup with Diane? It would explain a lot of the "coincidences" that were really statistically highly improbable."

At that point, I think I lost Kay's attention. Okay, I was reaching, but that would explain a lot of things that occurred… if it were possible. I'm probably losing your attention here too, since you probably think my mind went on sabbatical, at least temporarily.

Kay and I finished lunch, she gave me a hug, and we went our separate ways. I didn't plan on seeing her again, and at this point I still haven't seen her for over eighteen months. We've texted a few times to say *hi*, but that's about it. About six weeks before I saw Kay that day, I wrote this:

The Angel and the Rose

Long ago,
The Rose promised to help me
To be there when I need
I had no idea she'd passed
Four years ago it seems

Before I knew who she was
The Angel caught my eye
Did the Rose send the Angel to me
To help me in my life?

Having known both of them
I'm the one who knows
These two seem one in the same
The Angel and the Rose

The Rose held me in her heart
Until the very end
The Angel sees me only as
Someone who's just a friend

The look, the style, just who they are
They seem one in the same
It's time to let the Angel go
The Rose I hope remains

May 24, 2019

    If I do see Kay again, I'll give her the three poems I wrote about her in 2017 as well as "The Angel and the Rose."

    Okay, so have you had enough of the supernatural, mystical, coincidences? Well, guess what? I wasn't done with it. Three days after I saw Kay, I did something that I'd set up in late May. It's something I'd always wanted to do just one time, and now was as good a time as any to do it. I had a sit down with a medium, a psychic.

Chapter Thirteen

I had a sit down with a medium, named Sarah. She'd done domestic as well as international conferences and is fairly well known. It was a thirty-minute session that I was able to record the audio.

All Sarah wanted to know was the person's first name and their relationship to me. I asked about four people. My paternal grandparents, one of my best friends growing up Sal (yeah, Big Sal passed away about ten years earlier), and a "friend" named Zorina.

The first thing Sarah would do with each one was describe the area of the body that caused each one to pass on, then she'd get into other details. She was pretty good on my grandparents.

When she got to Sal she said, "He's taking responsibility for his passing."

She didn't specify what ailment he died from, and here's the reason why. Sal died from complications of diabetes. He didn't control his diet. He'd been overweight since we were kids. So, he took responsibility. She also keyed in on his being a funny guy, that he had lots of people around him, but that he was very sad inside. All of that was true since his business was being a professional comedian.

Then, Zorina was last. I had only stated that she was a friend. The first thing Sarah did was to place her right hand on her right-side abdomen below the rib cage.

She said, "Zorina is saying she feels sick to her stomach…it feels like chemo. Yes. She says it's chemo, and I get very ill."

I just sat there with no expression or reaction. I just watched and listened. Sarah was right on the money with what she was saying. Then, Sarah kind of hesitated like she was trying to gather and interpret something.

She said to me, "She's saying there are a lot of good memories with you like you were more than just a friend. Were you more than just friends?"

I had to finally acknowledge to Sarah that we were more than just friends.

I don't know how Sarah does what she does, but she does it very well. She was able to connect with the personalities of the four people I asked about. In particular, she had been very in tune with Sal's character, but then he was always a bigger than life and a physically imposing guy anyway.

Once again, I thought about that quote from Hamlet:

"There are more things in Heaven and earth Horatio, than are dreamt of in your philosophy."

So…do you still think I'm making more out of this hocus pocus and coincidence stuff than is necessary? If so, that's up to you and your personal beliefs. I've just been giving you the facts. You can draw your own conclusions as I have. Just remember one thing. I was there. I lived it.

In an email that I sent to Jeannette in mid-July '19, I gave her the dates that I planned to be in NY so we could get together. I also mentioned that I was planning to take a side trip to Puerto Rico for just a couple of days to pay my respects to Zorina. If Z had found me when she was sick, there wasn't anything in this world that could have kept me from going to her, to be with her in her final days. In the last weeks of her life, she wanted to try to find me, to see me one last time. Now that I'd found her, I was going to go to her.

As you already know, Zorina and I discussed marriage five times, the last of which was a promise to each other to "get married someday when the time was right." Now that Z was no longer here, I wanted to keep that promise in a symbolic way. By early August, I'd fulfilled that promise the only way I could. I'll discuss what I did during my get together with Jeannette and Little Zorina.

I hadn't set up my flights yet. I was still working on that. Jeannette emailed me back that she and her husband own a condo on the north shore of Puerto Rico just a few miles west of the airport. She offered to let me and anyone who traveled with me to stay there. I had no idea she had a place down there. I accepted and was so grateful for her offer and hospitality. I advised her that I would be making the trip alone. For me this wasn't a vacation…it was more of a pilgrimage to try to come to terms with Zorina's passing and to somehow let Z know that, if I had to, I'd travel to the ends of the earth for her.

After I'd met with Sarah, I just didn't have it in me anymore to date, and I had no desire to see or talk to anyone outside of the necessity to deal with people where I work. If friends contacted me, I was okay with that, but I pretty much stopped initiating contacting people. I was only calling my parents every couple of weeks just to touch base with them. I just wanted to be left alone. Between my job and getting the house organized, I was pretty busy anyway.

September arrived, and I was looking forward to seeing family and friends in NY. It had been over two years since I was there. The wedding was fun, and I got to stay with my parents for a few days and a couple of more days at my cousin James and his wife Guinevere's house. Yep, Guinevere. She's from England.

The day after the wedding, I was going to meet Jeannette and Little Z. I had last seen both of them over thirty-one years earlier on the day that Zorina had taken the photo of me pushing two-year old Little Z in the swing. I was a little nervous and a bit anxious to see both of them. There was so much that I wanted to tell them and so much, as well, that I wanted to know.

Sunday September 29th, 2019

After the wedding, James, his wife, and I went back to their house. We ended up having a few drinks and catching up on life. James and I reminisced a bit about our younger days which of course included him asking me to join him on a cold dark March evening forty-three years earlier. We finally called it a night at about three a.m.

I was hoping I didn't oversleep, since I had to meet Jeannette and Little Z at one o'clock for lunch at a restaurant in northern New Jersey. It was only about a thirty-minute drive from James' house to the restaurant. It was a really nice day with a cool breeze.

Jeannette and Little Z had already arrived and gotten a table on the outdoor patio. I nervously walked through the restaurant and opened the door to the patio area. About fifty feet straight ahead, I saw a woman stand up and smile. It was Jeannette.

The last time I'd seen her she was just twenty years old. The last time I'd seen Little Zorina, she was just a baby. She sure was a lot taller than the last time I saw her!

Jeannette and I gave each other a big hug and said hello. Little Z and I did the same. We ordered some drinks and a few appetizers to get us started. We began with some small talk about how nice a day it was and the wedding I went to the night before.

I brought three poems with me that I'd written since I'd mailed her the binder of poetry, photos, and copies of her mom's cards and letters. The three poems were "My Long Lost Love" and "My Rose of San Sebastian" that I already mentioned and a very short one that I'd just written a few weeks before my trip. Here's that last one:

One morning,
Should I awaken to find you lying next to me…
I'll know that I left this earth
And joined you in Heaven.

September 7, 2019

Then, we began to talk about where I had been for the last thirty-plus years and why I set out to find Zorina. In my initial conversation with Jeannette on the evening that we spoke in early March, we covered quite a bit during what was about a forty-five-minute conversation. What I didn't speak to that evening on the phone was what happened in June of '76.

It wasn't something that I wanted to do over the phone. Now, Little Z was there and we were in a public place. I told them the same things that you've already read in the first few chapters. There was the initial evening Z and I met, our first date, and those first few months when we were so happy together. I explained why I was going to end the relationship, a relationship that I didn't want to end just as much as Zorina didn't want it to end.

The only thing I said about June '76 was this, "Things got bad, very bad. I hurt your mom very much by telling her I thought we should stop seeing each other. It wasn't good, not good at all."

It was neither the time nor the place to get into that conversation. I asked some round about questions of Jeannette to see if she might have any knowledge of what had happened that June, but she didn't seem to know anything about it. At one point, I mentioned June of '82 and how, less than a week before my wedding, Zorina said to me that if I changed my mind about getting married, we'd go back out again and then we'd get married.

When I finished that story, Jeannette said her mom had shared that story with her. So, we got caught up on me and the twelve years that Zorina and I were both in NY. We also spoke about Jeannette's and Little Z's lives and what they were currently doing.

Jeannette brought Zorina's cell phone with her. She'd kept it since there were photos and even a few-minute video of Zorina on it from a few years before she passed away. I was able to see Zorina and listen to her voice in her later years in that video. She was as beautiful as ever. My eyes started to well up a bit, so I had to get hold of my emotions. We were on that patio and there were people at the other tables.

Then, I asked about Zorina and what had happened with her after mid-1988. I told Jeannette the last I knew was that her mom was married to Juan, pregnant, having the baby very soon, and she was living in California.

Jeannette then filled me in on things. Zorina had lost the baby very late in the pregnancy. She was almost forty years old when that happened. Then she got pregnant again in '89 and had a miscarriage. Her marriage to Juan began falling apart by late '89 and by mid '90 she was divorced and back in NY. Zorina would stay in NY and get married one more time.

Then she told me her mom was buried under her maiden name. Z had been married four times, once before I met her and three more times after we dated. When Jeannette told me all that, I just sat there stunned. Mine and Zorina's marriages had both basically come to an end by early 1990. She was headed back to NY, and I was just starting a relationship with Diane halfway across the country. The promise that we'd made on the bench on the boardwalk at the amusement park in August of '87, that we'd get married when the time was right, had arrived by early 1990, but neither one of us knew what was happening with the other since we'd lost touch by '89.

It was at this point that I decided to share with Jeannette the symbolic gesture regarding the promise that Zorina and I had made to each other about getting married someday. I was going to place the item I had at Z's grave when I went to Puerto Rico, but I removed it from my pocket and handed it to Jeannette for her to keep.

There are businesses that make custom military style dog tags with any inscription that you want to have put on them. I had two identical sets of dog tags made. I wear one all the time and a second set that I had just given to Jeannette. The inscription reads as follows on both sets:

MICHAEL AVELLINO
ZORINA AVELLINO
OUR PROMISES KEPT
FROM AUG 1987 AT
THE AMUSEMENT PARK

As a symbolic gesture to keep our promises to each other, I had given Zorina my last name, not knowing that she requested to be buried under her maiden name, not under one of her husband's names. At some point in time, she should have been my wife. As far as I was concerned, I now felt justified in my decision to have that inscription put on the tags.

We talked some more about what went on over the years. There had been some smiles, some laughs, and of course a few tears. It was now pushing five o'clock.

Things seemed to be winding down for us, so I picked up the tab. We sat there a few more minutes finishing our drinks, and we were still talking about things.

Then, Jeannette said, "I want to have another drink. Do you want to have another? Can you stay?"

I said, "Sure. I can stay."

The three of us ended up being there another two and a half hours. We managed to cover memories of other things about Z and me that had happened over the years. One of the things that Jeannette spoke about was her mom thinking she might want to try to find me in the late '90's or early 2000's, but Zorina didn't pursue it.

I've wondered if Z didn't try to find me because she might have been leery of the possibility that I might have died. Remembering how she'd felt about me in our early days, I wondered if she might have been afraid to face that possibility. I know that it would have been as difficult for her to find out that I was gone as it has been for me to accept that about her. I really don't know the answer to that question. It's just a possibility that I've considered.

It was about 7:30 now, and it was getting dark out. I picked up the tab from our second round. Jeannette gave me the keys to her condo in Puerto Rico. The three of us took a few photos together and said our goodbyes. I thanked Jeannette for the use of her condo and headed back to James' place.

It had been quite a day. I hadn't been sure of what to expect or how it would go. As it turned out, everything went so well. Zorina must have told Jeannette quite a bit about our relationship, possibly a bit more than Jeannette let on. However, the details of what occurred in June '76 didn't seem to have been shared.

I got back to James' place, and we talked about my meeting with Jeannette and Little Z. Once again, we talked about the old days when we were younger and full of piss and vinegar. I got a good night's sleep, and the next day I went back to my parent's place for a few days.

On Wednesday, I headed to the airport and caught a flight to Puerto Rico. About four hours later, I landed in San Juan and rented a car.

The drive was only about ten minutes west to the condo. The highways in Puerto Rico are just as modern and well-kept as they are in the States, but those darn road signs are all in Spanish! Somehow, I managed to figure those out, but it took a few minutes extra to find the right address to the complex I was looking for.

There was a security gate to drive through and a specific space I had to park in. I took the elevator up to the 20th floor penthouse and entered the condo. It was a huge three bedroom that was probably upward of 1,700 sq ft. I looked around and thought about Zorina.

She had been here during her lifetime, and now I was here. The emotions just ran through me. I knew that the next day I would be within feet of her, and I still wouldn't be able to see her.

It was late afternoon, so I went out for a bite to eat and tried to send texts to a few people to let them know I arrived safely, but my phone wouldn't communicate. When I'd met with Jeannette, I told her I wanted to buy flowers for her mom. She advised me that real ones would wilt in the heat in a day and that silk flowers were a better choice.

I stopped in a local store, and they had some smaller artificial sweetheart roses. I bought five of those, one for each time that Zorina and I had discussed marriage.

Once I got back to the condo, I got on the wi-fi there and was able to text and make calls. I searched the web for directions to the cemetery and wrote everything down. I hoped I would make it to my destination as planned, but I was somewhere I'd never been, with road signs I had to interpret, and it was about eighty miles west to the cemetery. I'd come all this way, and I was determined to make it to Zorina's resting place.

October 3rd , 2019

I was on the road by nine o'clock. I got on the main highway, and the first forty miles or so were a breeze. I had to take another highway southwest for about twenty miles. Then came the roads through small towns.

At one point, I wasn't sure if I'd gone too far and missed a turn or if I hadn't gone far enough. I pulled into a gas station and tried to speak to a couple of people, but don't ya know…they only spoke Spanish!

A *Pepsi* delivery truck pulled in, and I approached the driver, hoping he spoke English. He did…just enough for me to ask where San Sebastian was. He let me know it was still about twenty miles ahead. I have to tell you that I thanked him profusely!

The final few miles were on tight winding roads. The road I was on ended, and I had to make a left or a right. Don't forget, my phone wasn't working, so I couldn't look on the internet. I pulled into a gas station to ask which way it was to the cemetery. Well, they didn't speak English either!

I had the name of the cemetery and a phone number for the grounds keeper, named Alejandro. The guy at the station called the number and spoke to him. He gestured to me to follow him in his car. Within about three minutes, we pulled into the cemetery. Yeah…I thanked that guy profusely too!

Then I met Alejandro there. Guess what…he didn't speak English either! Here it is 2019, Puerto Rico has been a Commonwealth of the U.S. for decades. and you get out of San Juan and almost nobody speaks English! What's up with that?

It took a few minutes for me to get Alejandro to understand the grave I was looking for, but he finally understood. As we walked down a couple of paths to get there, it was beginning to hit me that I was about to be as near to Zorina as I'd been in over thirty-one years. He pointed out the tomb to me. Along with Zorina, her mother, and her daughter, Gigi, are both interred in that same tomb. Alejandro kept Z's tomb, at Jeannette's request, very clean and orderly. I thanked him for leading me to it.

I placed the five roses at the head of the grave with the other silk roses that were there. I'd also brought the last three poems "My Long Lost Love", "My Rose of San Sebastian", and the "One Morning" poem and wrapped them around the roses I'd brought. I told her that I still loved her, and I'd searched for her, hoping we could finally be together.

I said I was sorry for hurting her, and I never meant for that to happen that way, and that if I had known she was looking for me in her final days that I would have been there for her. I told her why we'd lost touch with each other. It was a very emotional visit to her resting place.

As I was leaving, I thanked Alejandro very much for his help. As I drove away, a calm came over me. In February, when I had set out to find her, I had no idea things would turn out the way they did. Seven months and 2,700 miles later, I stood before her in her resting place and told her I would return to see her again. And I will.

The drive back to San Juan went pretty quick. I got back by about two-thirty. I decided to go down to the beach just behind the condo, since I hadn't been to the ocean in over twenty-five years. I took an empty plastic bottle with me to put some sand in.

There weren't many people on the beach that afternoon. I went into the water just up to my knees and I looked out at the vast Atlantic. I walked up and down the beach a bit looking for seashells, found quite a few and put them in my pocket. I looked down the beach in both directions hoping I'd magically see Zorina walking toward me. We'd had so many wonderful times together at the beaches in New York.

My New Year's Eve resolution to go to a beach in 2019 had actually come true, and I had Z to thank for it. I took one last look down the beach and gathered my things together. When I got back to the condo, I called Jeannette to let her know how the day went. We talked for a while, and I thanked her for everything she'd done for me.

She said, "I hope you're able to get some closure with mom."

I replied, "The only way I'll get closure with Zorina is when we're together again on the other side."

Then, I finally remembered to ask Jeannette about the ring that I had given Zorina in 1983, the ring Z wanted me to give her to wear while we were dating in 1976 with my initials engraved on it. I explained to her that my grandparents had given me the ring for my Catholic Confirmation when I was eight years old. Jeannette said she'd have to take a look for it, and she'd get back to me. I supposed she still had some of Zorina's personal things and would have to look through them.

After I spoke to Jeannette, I called my buddy Ray and his wife Irene, and we talked for a while. He said the same thing to me about closure, and my reply to him was the same as I'd said to Jeannette.

I had a long day ahead of me on Friday to get home with a stopover in Chicago. When I got home, I placed some of the sand I'd collected into a small glass bottle. That, along with a couple of seashells, a few photos of Z and me, and some mementos I'd kept since '76, and excerpts from a couple of things we'd written to and about each other. I placed all of them into a shadow box.

The morning after I returned home, I got a text from Jeannette with a photo she had just taken of the ring.

> **JEANNETTE:** I believe this is your ring and feel you should have it.

I texted back:

> Oh, Jeannette. You have it. I'm shaking.

I wasn't sure if Zorina would still have it after all those years. Jeannette said she would mail it to me, and a few days later it arrived. I opened the envelope. The ring was in a ring case. I opened the case and took the ring out and just looked at it for a minute. I didn't put it on, and I haven't put it on since I got it from Jeannette. I placed it with the shadow box and other mementos I kept from our relationship. I had given it to Zorina as a symbol of my love for her. It's her ring and now I just happen to be in possession of it.

My son Mickey was always a good kid, very polite and well mannered. He kind of took after me in that way. Nearly six years ago, he married a girl who was a few years older than him, divorced, and had two kids from a previous marriage. He'd told me about her when they were still dating. I kept my nose out of his business while he was dating her, and now they have two kids of their own together.

About a month after I got back from Puerto Rico, I spoke to him. I told him I was proud of him for making the choice he did about marrying someone in that situation. I didn't elaborate on why I said what I said. I was just happy for him that his marriage was successful and that he and his wife were very happy together.

In mid '20, my daughter Helen came to visit me for about a week. She saw the shadow box and asked me who the woman was. I told her I'd explain it to her the day before she returned home. That day arrived, and I had a talk with her and told her, in metaphorical terms, that both her mom and I, and Diane and I, had finished our dances, and that Zorina and I didn't get to do that.

Then I told her about my trip to Puerto Rico and about June of '76. When I was done telling her, she just sat there and didn't say a word.

I said to her, "I can see you weren't expecting that kind of story."

She understood the depth and the seriousness of my relationship that I'd had with Zorina.

Chapter Fourteen

I've had numerous emails and a couple of conversations with Jeannette since my trip eighteen months ago. There just somehow seems to still be things that we talk about regarding Zorina that are new and enlightening to both of us. I found out that Jeannette had written a lengthy and detailed obituary about her mom when she passed away, so I'd like to share some of it with you:

The beautiful Zorina passed on at the age of 66, although we all know she was really 21. She departed in her favorite city of New York after a graceful courageous battle with cancer. The last words she heard were telling her how much we love her and the last touch she felt were our arms embracing her. Zorina was born in San Sebastian, Puerto Rico.

Her childhood was shared with numerous cousins playing in the countryside and running through the sugarcane fields. As she explained, their entertainment was strategizing how they were going to shoot a tiny bird, cook it and divide it between 20 kids. She greatly appreciated getting a single penny and a few pieces of candy for Christmas. Her mother worked very hard in the United States and soon sent her a plane ticket to New York City, forever making her a native New Yorker.

Forever, determined to conquer the world and enjoy everything in it, she started her journey as a devoted single mother in 1970. With a High School education, a belief nothing is impossible, a heart filled with endless love, forgiveness and compassion for everyone, she not only raised and taught her children how to be generous and humble and how to feel unconditionally loved and appreciated, but every person she met as well.

Her home was always filled with people, and she made every person feel special, acknowledged, and most importantly loved. Zorina was a vibrant spirit that screamed out "let's have fun!" Her famous words were "Shake what your mother gave you" and "So you know better". She was always smiling, always dancing and always having a party or a barbeque. Her friends loved her, the men loved her even more and her family will love her forever.

She was a devoted mother, a very entertaining grandmother, dedicated great grandmother, a sister, a Titi, a cousin, a wife, a daughter-in-law, a mother-in-law, sister-in-law, a confidant, a friend, an amazing unforgettable woman and everything, everything, everything to us. So many were touched during her short life. Her legacy - that forgiveness is always possible, to love everyone unconditionally, always help if you can, to always say "I Love You" when leaving and to always make sure you have lipstick on.

Zorina asked to give a special message to her family and friends after learning of her terminal cancer - Please forgive me for not telling you sooner of my illness, but I only wanted to save you from the pain. Your smiles are what kept me going and helped breath more life into my body that was failing me. I lived a great life and I have no regrets. Please try not to cry for me. Remember how beautiful I was, my spirit for life and have a great time at my funeral. My daughter promised me I would be in a hot red sexy dress and my favorite music would be playing. I love you all so much I feel my heart is going to burst. I'm going to miss you so much, but I'm finally going to be joining my mother, my daughter "Gigi", my baby boy "Carlos" and all my dear family and friends that are waiting for me. I'm not scared, I'll be getting heaven ready for you all. Don't want to see you anytime soon. And don't forget, I'll be visiting you every once in a while. During her last 10 days in the hospital, a little girl kept visiting her. Only she could see her.

Her son and daughter believe the little girl was their sister "Gigi". So, Zorina was never alone, while we were letting her go in the physical, "Gigi" was welcoming her in the spiritual.

There was one other thing that Zorina wrote as well before she passed away that I mentioned earlier:

When I leave you don't weep for me. Pass the wine around and remember how my laughing pleased you. Look at one another smiling and don't forget about touching. Sing the songs I loved best and dance one time all together. As for me, I'll be off, running somewhere on the beach. When you're ready I'll be there – waiting for you. Take your time.

At the beginning of the book, I stated, as of right now, I can't say with any certainty that the story I'm about to tell you is over. It all depends on your personal beliefs.

I also stated, both the Bible and a quote from Shakespeare's play Hamlet have always made me wonder if this world we're born into, and we die in is just the beginning of our existence in this universe. The Bible, like nearly every religion, says there is life after death.

Shakespeare's quote once again:

"There are more things in Heaven and earth Horatio, than are dreamt of in your philosophy."

As I'm writing these last few thoughts, it's Sunday, Valentine's Day 2021. I know you may be thinking how unbelievably convenient that may be. Fact is, I only had the last two chapters to write, and I've been in the house all weekend because the temperature never reached ten degrees outside in the area that I live.

Friday March 5th will be forty-five years to the day that we went on our first date. Zorina was right when she gave me the record "You'll Never Find Another Love Like Mine." As well, I'm really hoping she was right when she played "Someday We'll Be

Together" on the jukebox for me.

She's still in my heart and in my head. She's always been in my heart, that's a given. The only way to limit her presence in my head is for me to fall in love again. Zorina was my first love. The way things are going she may very well be my last.

We never had a Christmas or a Thanksgiving together. We never had a Fourth of July, a Labor Day weekend, or a vacation together. What we did have was each other, and in both of our hearts, we always knew that love would always be there. In my lifetime, no one and nothing, has affected me the way she did and still does.

Based on my own personal beliefs, I don't think this story is over. I have a feeling I'll be seeing Zorina again. My inner "Richie" is still there after all these years. That wide-eyed, innocent kid who had a fantasy come true still believes that miracles can happen and that a string of related coincidences are more than just coincidences. Maybe Shakespeare was right, after all.

Just a reminder about one other thing that I've already told you about myself. I'm a hopeless romantic and a sentimental fool… always have been and always will be.

• • • • • • • •

Does Heaven really exist?

If it does, then, in my last moments on this earth, I'll hear a voice or voices, not being able to distinguish them. There will be a moment of darkness, but soon after there'll be a ray of light in the distance.

As I walk toward that light, I'll hear a rushing sound. I'll find myself on a beach, and the sound is that of the ocean waves meeting the shore. The sun is on the horizon, but I'm not sure if it's sunrise or sunset. As well, I'm not sure what this place is or why I'm here.

In the distance, someone is on the edge of the water, looking out toward the sea. I get closer and I see that it's Zorina…my *munequita.*

She turns in my direction and begins running. A few feet from me she stops, then she takes a few very slow steps toward me. I reach out my hand, and she places her hand in mine. I pull her toward me, hold her close, and she looks up at me with those big dark eyes.

I lean over slightly, and she gets up on her toes, and we kiss for a few seconds. Then she lays her head on my chest, and we just live in the moment.

This all seems very familiar to me from sometime in my past, only this time it won't last for just a few minutes. We look into each other's eyes, and we smile. Then, we walk hand in hand along the shore, together now, and forever more.